Taming Crazy

Confessions and Lessons

Taming Crazy
Confessions and Lessons

ALICYA PERREAULT

CARSAM

for Ger

Contents

Introduction

I used to think the older you got, the more self-assured you became. This, of course, is complete and utter bollocks!

My life had been full of *barely holding it together* moments, but I had become so good at concealing it—so accustomed to hiding behind a façade—that nobody knew just how close to the edge I had become. Including me.

Worrying, over-thinking, over-analyzing, and obsessive thoughts defined me. It was who I was. It was something I often joked about with those who knew me best. But behind the fragile smile and witty comebacks, was someone I didn't fully recognize anymore.

Worry and anxiety had gradually seeped into every pore. It flowed through my bloodstream, enveloped every muscle, and wrapped itself around every bone. I lay awake at night, tossing and turning, praying for the few hours of protection that sleep could offer. I wanted it to swallow me whole. To put an end to the continuous thoughts that circled my brain for hours on end. I was emotionally, mentally, and physically exhausted, but most of all, I was afraid.

I had always been an over-thinker—a worrier—it was part of my identity. It was something I thought I could keep hidden from the outside world. I became an expert at pretending to be *normal* (or at least what I thought *normal* should look like.)

I was unaware that the constant worry that crippled me— the fear that something was about to go terribly wrong, or the endless excuses I could conjure up to stop moving forward in my life—were clear signs that something wasn't right. I thought it was normal to worry. But there is a vast difference between the usual 'run of the mill' worry and my completely illogical 'the sky is falling, and we're all going to die a horrible death' kind of worry.

Who knew?

The thing about anxiety and depression is that it sneaks up on you. You don't see it coming. You don't want to see it. It seeps into all the cracks and takes root in the darkness. It's in-sidious. It views any setback or perceived failure you experi-ence, as an opportunity to tighten its grip—and once it has you—it makes you retreat further inside yourself. Unfortu-nately, that's just what it wants. It wants to find you alone in the darkness so it can feed off your insecurities, worries, and fears. (Sounds a bit dramatic, doesn't it?)

Depression and anxiety are liars.

They're pathological.

Experiencing them together is like falling into a black hole filled with quicksand. You can struggle, but every thought you have pulls you deeper into the darkness. All those thoughts are lies dressed up as doubt.

Depression devoid of anxiety leaves you deflated. Like a discarded balloon left in the gutter. Useless. Unworthy.

People are often surprised to learn about my anxiety because they assume they would have been able to see the signs. They don't realize that most of us have pretty good ninja skills when it comes to hiding what we're really feeling. The last thing we want is attention, especially when we're already feeling like a complete nut. We may not be hyperventilating or breathing into a paper bag, but that doesn't mean we are not experiencing intense anxiety or panic on the inside. (I blame Hollywood for the paper bag thing.)

What made everything worse was my undiagnosed Obsessive-Compulsive Disorder. I had always believed that OCD showed up as physical obsessions and compulsions that interfered with daily life. I didn't wash my hands three hundred times a day. I didn't meticulously clean my house, in fact, I do everything I can to avoid cleaning the house. (Although I do have a thing about Q-tips and locking my vehicle, and some other stuff.) What I didn't know, was that my obsessions and compulsions were just as debilitating. They affected me greatly and took the form of disturbing thoughts and worries that were excessive, irrational, and illogical. I was performing continuous rituals in my head to try and dispel these thoughts. I took this as clear evidence I was going mad.

By the Fall of 2014, I found myself successfully managing my emotional health and my debilitating anxiety attacks. At first, I thought it was a fluke. I thought I was fooling myself and that what I believed to be the successful management of my anxiety—was merely a reprieve. I thought sooner or later it would be back with a vengeance. Mocking me. Rejoicing in the fact it had fooled me.

Anxiety is a sadistic bitch!

For years, I thought I was the only one who felt the way I did. The only one whose body betrayed her. The only one who couldn't get through the day without obsessing over some stupid little thing. The older I got, the crazier I felt. I thought it was only a matter of time before I became so utterly bat-shit crazy that my darling husband, Ger, would have no choice but to have me committed.

Generalized anxiety disorder (GAD) is one of the most commonly diagnosed disorders in the world, so I knew I couldn't be the only one thinking that they were alone in their struggles with it. The problem was I didn't know anyone personally who suffered from it. Of course, now I know we're all just bloody good at hiding it.

We don't all experience anxiety, depression, panic attacks or OCD the same way. We are all unique with our own methods of handling (or not handling) our emotional and mental pain. One person's anxiety or depression is not necessarily better or worse than another's.

Your experiences will be different from mine.

But we all have one thing in common—we suffer!

I'm sharing my story in the hope it will help you. Climbing out of the rabbit hole takes courage, strength, and tears. I've been in the trenches and know how it feels to live there. I know what it's like to feel so hopeless that you don't even know if there is a light at the end of the tunnel, let alone how you will find the strength to find this light.

"I can't write a book!" I replied when my sister first suggested I write one.

"Why not?" she asked.

I could already sense a million reservations building up inside me, (okay, maybe not a million but at least three to start with.) The biggest one—the one that kept coming up repeatedly—was what I'd imagine everyone else would be thinking.

Who does she think she is?

This was something I'd battled my whole life. It was the voice in my head I had always listened to. At times, it could be loud and unyielding, other times it would be a whisper.

Who do you think you are?

I did have a lot to say—at times I had too much to say—but I needed time to find my voice. I needed to be standing so far away from that damn rabbit hole that I no longer feared the fall. I needed enough space between who I once was and the person I had now become.

Who do you think you are?

With help from Brene Brown's *Daring Greatly*, I put on my big girl knickers, grabbed a pen and started writing.

This is my story.

"It is not the critic who counts; not the man who points out how the strong man stumbles, or where the doer of deeds could have done them better. The credit belongs to the man who is actually in the arena, whose face is marred by dust and sweat and blood; who strives valiantly; who errs, who comes short again and again, because there is no effort without error and shortcoming; but who does actually strive to do the deeds; who knows great enthusiasms, the great devotions; who spends himself in a worthy cause; who at the best knows in the end the triumph of high achievement, and who at the worst, if he fails, at least fails while daring greatly, so that his place shall never be with those cold and timid souls who neither know victory nor defeat.."

~ Theodore Roosevelt ('Man in the Arena' April 23, 1910)

1. The Beginning of The End

This is it. I've gone mad.

"Are you okay?" Ger asked, tossing his coat on the living room chair. It was close to suppertime, and I was slumped on the sofa, still in my pyjamas surrounded by a mountain of soggy tissues.

"I'm okay," I managed to whisper before bursting out in big ugly sobs. Again.

"You're not okay. What happened?" he asked, sitting down beside me and wrapping his arms around me. This of course, just made everything. So. Much. Worse.

I continued to cry big, ugly, heaving sobs into his chest leaving a large wet spot on his crisp blue linen shirt. I kept sobbing until I was… sobless.

"I don't know what's wrong with me. I think I've finally gone mad."

The tears fell faster than I could mop them up. My eyes, cheeks, and nose were red and raw which made me wish I had bought those lovely soft tissues with the moisturizer built in, instead of the cheap generic ones.

It had taken everything I had to drag myself out of bed that morning. I was exhausted and didn't have the energy to comb my hair, let alone change out of my pyjamas. As I poured myself a cup of coffee, my mind was racing. I couldn't seem to shake the feeling of despair. A heavy blanket of uneasiness had enveloped me and without warning—I had burst out crying.

What the hell?

I felt ridiculous. I had no logical reason or even the slightest clue as to why I was crying—and no matter how hard I tried— I couldn't stop the tears from falling. And falling.

It wasn't until Ger came home from work and saw the blubbering mess on the sofa in place of his wife that I realized I hadn't moved all day. All I could do was sit and wait for the darkness of night when I could migrate from the living room to the bedroom. As if staying up until dark was a personal triumph of some sort. Sinking into bed, I fell asleep almost instantly, which was rare but welcoming. I slept soundly through the night and when I woke the next morning—much later than usual—I was disappointed to discover that I felt exactly the same as I did the day before.

Why the hell didn't I feel any better?

Days passed as I continued to wallow in the depths of worry and despair. Wandering aimlessly between misery and melancholy. Between darkness and nothingness. My thinking was in overdrive and yet I felt numb. I was also angry. Angry for being weak. Angry at not being able to pull myself out of it. Most of all, I was angry with feeling out of control.

I had always been able to keep myself in check on the surface. To not let my anxieties, worries, and irrational fears see the light of day. I was the one people came to with their problems. I was the fixer. I was *Olivia Pope* for fuck's sake. So why couldn't I figure this out?

After three long days of emptiness, I picked up my phone and read my sister's last text message, 'WHAT THE HELL IS GOING ON? WHERE ARE YOU?'

I'd been ignoring everyone—including my sister—and I knew she wasn't going to let me get away with it much longer. She would be worrying, and I didn't want that. I just wanted to be left alone.

'I don't feel like talking right now.' I messaged back, hoping that would be enough.

'Why?' she replied, but I couldn't summon the strength to answer her. Within minutes my phone started ringing and ringing and ringing. I ignored it. I wanted to turn it off, go back to bed and hide under the covers, but I knew that with every ring I ignored I was just making things worse. I didn't want her to worry—but talking—talking was the last thing I wanted to do. I knew if I kept ignoring her, she would call Ger at work and he was already concerned about my mental state. I didn't want to add to that growing pile of concern. Reluctantly, I picked up the phone.

"What's wrong?" she said as soon as I answered.

"Nothing," I said, my voice cracking which I knew would do nothing to reassure her.

"I'm coming over," she said.

"No don't. I'm okay, really I am."

"You don't sound okay. I'm coming over."

"No. Please don't." I begged between sobs. "I can't handle company right now, not even yours. I'm okay. I'll be fine."

"Maybe you need to see your doctor."

"I can't right now."

"You can't, or you won't?"

"Can't. I will though. I promise."

"Why don't I believe you?"

"Seriously, I'll go. I just need to be over the worst of it first. You know me."

"Yes, I do. Which is why I'm going with you."

"Nope. Not necessary. Actually, I feel better already."

"Liar."

My tendency towards being anxious, melodramatic, and irrational was a running joke between my sister and me. I had always been the crazy one. The dramatic one. The one who could take the tiniest thing and turn it into something newsworthy. We often laughed about it, but even she didn't know just how deep the anxiety well ran, or how much it was beginning to terrify me.

Looking back, I think anxiety had always been my Achilles heel, I just didn't know there was a name for it. It would start with a familiar gnawing in the pit of my stomach. My heart would beat faster and harder as if in a desperate plea to escape my body. I would be paralyzed with endless thoughts hovering around my head like gulls circling a fishing trawler at sea. I never shared how I felt because I worried about what people would think of me. Although I always told myself I didn't care.

Describing anxiety to someone who has never experienced it is difficult. It's like a foreign language, and in all honesty, I didn't quite understand it myself. Anxiety is different for everyone, but what I did know, was what it felt like for me.

It's like swimming. At first, you're doing fine, floating in the calm shallows staring up at the big blue sky. Without warning a sense of uneasiness starts to surround you. No one else can see it or feel it, but you know it's there lurking just beneath the surface. At that moment, the only thing you know with any certainty is that you need to get out of the water.

You start swimming towards the shore, heading for solid ground. To everyone else, you appear calm and controlled— but underneath the surface—you're paddling for your life.

The harder and faster you swim, the further from safety you seem to get. With every stroke, you're pulled back into deeper, darker water until the cold, eerie blackness fully envelops you. Dragging you under. You struggle to keep your head above the surface while the sound of blood pumping through your head is deafening. You fight with everything you have to—just—keep—breathing. Your lungs scream for air as your heart thumps furiously in your chest. No one can see you're drowning. No one can hear your silent screams.

Emotionally and mentally exhausted, you manage to pull yourself to safety. You know you should be relieved to have made it through to the other side, but all you feel is shame.

Shame you couldn't be stronger.

Shame you couldn't be like everyone else.

And every time you get back in the water—every time you battle—you get a little bit weaker, and you can't help but wonder how close you are to losing it all.

Survival takes its toll.

Anxiety beats you down.

It erodes your sense of self.

It chews you up and spits you out.

If that sounds a bit dramatic, it's because it is.
In your head, the drama is as real as it gets.

From as far back as I can remember, I've had a love-hate relationship with my thoughts. I loved that I could be whisked away to places and worlds limited only by my imagination. But as I got older—the thoughts that used to take me to beautiful worlds—often led me to places I didn't want to go.

Dark, scary places.

As a child, my active imagination had often sheltered me from the harsh realities of life. But worry and anxiety had slowly crept in to take its place.

For many of us, growing up is not a smooth transition. It can be hard. It can be ruthless and leave us laying facedown in the dirt. Bruised, bloodied, and broken.

I'm not entirely sure when life dragged me from a world of colour into the greyness. But looking back, I can't remember a time when over-thinking wasn't a big part of my life. I over-thought everything and was often in such a state of chronic worry, it bordered on the neurotic. I'd always managed to fold it up neatly and tuck it away. Hiding it from the outside world.

It was my dirty little secret, and I guarded it closely.

I was careful not to share everything that was going on inside my head because my thoughts could often be dark and consuming. Perhaps it was a rare glimpse of optimism that had me believing it would get better over time. I thought age and experience would be my allies. I thought my future life would make more sense, but as I got older, the more irrational and illogical my thoughts became.

By the time I was well into my adult years, my anxiety and worry had hit an all-time high, and I began retreating from the world around me. I'd always been an introvert and was perfectly fine with that label. People drained me. There weren't many people I liked or felt comfortable enough to want to spend a whole lot of time with anyway, so I was more than happy in my introversion.

But this was much more than just being an introvert.

Anxiety had slowly taken over. It had seeped into every dark corner. It had wrapped itself around every thought, and every aspect of my life was now suffering.

I began avoiding social situations altogether and became one of those annoying people who say they will go to something and then made an excuse at the last minute not to show up. At the time, I thought my reasons were valid, but of course, they weren't. I always had good intentions of going. I wanted to be there, but when the time came—I couldn't do it.

I just couldn't.

There were always reasons why I couldn't or shouldn't go. I was a fully-fledged member of the *Extreme Introvert Club*, (no attendance required.) I was used to not wanting to *people,* but it had now morphed into something more. It had slowly developed into an acute form of social anxiety, and even though I knew introversion and anxiety were not mutually inclusive—I had both.

When Ger and I first moved to a new city, I joined a woman's social group. I had the notion that *normal* people had friends.

Lots of friends. And although it was entirely out of my comfort zone, I was determined to be that person. Whoever she is.

The first event I signed up for was a book club. I was going to nail book club. Books were my friends. I could do books with my eyes closed (you know what I mean.) The plan was to meet at a restaurant and discuss the book.

No problem. I can do that.

The book was the easy part, but of course, it didn't take long before I started over-thinking EVERYTHING. I wanted to sound smart and enlightened but not too clever. I wanted to come across as genuine and friendly. What I really wanted was a sense of how it felt to fit in and see what I had been missing all these years.

Googling the restaurant's menu, I memorized what to order. I knew exactly how long it would take to get there and calculated the time I should arrive. Not too early because being the first one there would be horrifying, but I also didn't want to be late. I needed to time it just right.

What if I'm too early, and I'm sitting alone?

What if I'm late?

Where will I sit and what if nobody sits next to me?

What if everyone there knows each other already?

Ignoring the voices in my head, I plugged the restaurant address into my GPS, and entered the organizer's cell number into my phone. I was prepared. I was going to do this.

Normal people did this all the time, so why couldn't I?

What could possibly go wrong?

This is good. I can do this, I thought, while trying to ignore the gnawing feeling deep down in the pit of my stomach which seemed to grow in intensity with every mile. My pulse raced, and the closer I got to my destination—the more nauseated I felt.

Breathe, just breathe.

I must be getting sick, I thought as I drove right past the restaurant. I kept driving and soon heard the familiar voice 'Recalculating' coming from the dashboard.

"Shut up, I know. Stop judging me!" I screamed at the GPS. I quickly turned the car around, but instead of looking for a place to park—I headed home.

"Hey honey," I announced as I walked into the living room, dropping a big bag of junk food on the sofa. I had stopped and picked up snacks on the way home because I'm thoughtful like that (although I'm guessing it was more like guilt and shame that had led me up the snack aisle.)

"I changed my mind. Wanna watch a movie instead?"

"Sounds great," Ger replied, and I thought I saw a flicker of a smile on his face.

I fooled myself into thinking I'd just changed my mind or didn't feel like going. But Ger knew me well. He's also smart enough not to let me know that he knew what I was doing. I always had a good excuse for not showing up.

Excuses. I was full of them, and they served me well.

Until they didn't.

Gradually, I started making excuses for not going any-where. Ger took over the grocery shopping, and I told myself it was because he enjoyed it, or at least didn't hate it as much as I did. We even discovered grocery shopping from home. All I had to do was order everything with a few clicks on the computer, and Ger picked it up the next day. It was genius!

They deliver it to your door now. It's like they know.

When I did have to venture out, my internal dialogue began its usual routine.

Where will I go to get everything I need?

How will I get there?

What time should I go?

Do I have enough gas?

What will I wear?

My hair looks terrible.

I don't feel good.

Do I really need to go today?

I don't think I need to go.

I do need to buy hair dye, but maybe it can wait.

I don't need to dye my roots if I part my hair differently.

I wish I could wear hats.

Maybe Ger can go for me when he get's off work.

I don't feel good.

I'm not going.

With that decision, I felt better immediately. Until an hour or two later when I started thinking I should have gone and felt guilty and stupid. Again.

I even avoided going across the street to check the mailbox.

What if I bumped into a neighbour and had to talk to them?

The easiest solution was to not go to the mailbox. So, I stopped going. Ger started picking up the mail on his way home from work. It didn't seem like a big deal at the time, but all these little insignificant things were beginning to add up.

It was during this time that I also began to feel lost and out of balance. It wasn't as if I had ever felt *normal*, but now I was feeling out of control too. And if there's one thing that can send me over the edge—it's knowing I have no control. I had read somewhere that chronic anxiety sufferers are quite often control-freaks. If this was true, then crown me queen. Controlling a situation helped quell the fear of the unknown and help mitigate the *What Ifs*.

Being out of control without knowing why was a whole new ballgame for me, and I didn't know the rules, let alone how to play.

I had always been able to navigate my way around my worry and anxiety and be able to push it aside. I could even ignore it to some degree, but this was something more. I was having trouble finding my way through, and my usual anxiety took on a heaviness that I couldn't shrug off.

What I didn't realize at the time, was that I had fallen into an unfamiliar state of depression, and it pushed me into unknown territory.

It terrified me.

I felt like I was stuck at the bottom of a deep well and from where I was sitting—I could no longer see the sky.

Taming Crazy

2. Reaching Out

It has nothing to do with being brave or courageous.
It's about holding on for dear life.

"How are you today Alicya?" she asked, sitting at her impeccably tidy desk.

She had struggled with my name which wasn't that unusual. People had been butchering my name for as long as I can remember, but she didn't ask me to correct her like most people usually did. So, I didn't.

My eyes darted around the dimly lit room as I sank into the large grey sofa that almost took up one entire wall of the small office. It was a surprisingly comfy sofa. Yet despite its softness, I was feeling extremely uncomfortable. I was completely out of my element as they say, although I'm not entirely sure what my element is. I'm a Scorpio, so maybe water?

I could feel my heart pounding beneath my t-shirt as if it was trying to escape the confines of my chest. Taking a few deep breaths, I tried to settle myself down as best I could and hoped my inner turmoil didn't reflect too much on the outside. She smiled, and I attempted to smile back but felt the slight twitch on the right side of my mouth which meant it probably looked more like a grimace.

Pull yourself together Alicya, get a grip!

Inhaling deeply, I caught the subtle aroma of lavender emanating from a well-used candle on her desk. Its flame flickered violently as if it was desperately trying to save itself from drowning in the liquid wax that had pooled around its wick. I knew how it felt.

The room was windowless. The only light coming from a large table lamp sitting on a glass table tucked in next to the sofa. It gave the look and feel of a friendly home office instead of the stark, clinical room on the fourth floor of an old brick professional building. As I glanced around the room, my eyes suddenly caught hers, and from the curious look on her face, I could tell she was waiting for me to respond.

Damn, I really need to pay attention. I bet it will be the first note she scribbles down in my file. 'Doesn't pay attention. Easily distracted.'

I had resisted any kind of clinical therapy up until now for reasons I'm not entirely sure of. Perhaps seeking therapy made it all too real. Perhaps I wasn't ready to admit to someone that I was failing, especially when I couldn't admit it to myself. I'd been advocating for mental health services for years. Encouraging other people to reach out for help, yet I wasn't ready to face it myself. Admitting I needed help took more courage than I thought I had. I wasn't sure I was brave enough. But, here I was—a therapy virgin—sitting in the middle of a surprisingly comfortable sofa in a therapist's office. I was under some delusion that just by being there, in that room, on that

sofa, would somehow make me feel a little better. I was wrong.
Should I be laying down or did that only happen in movies?
What do I do with all these damn cushions?
Is this a test? Are these cushions a metaphor for something?

Booking the appointment had been difficult, but I told myself
I needed to give this one hundred percent effort. I was going
to be honest about how I was feeling and be open to her sug-
gestions. Most of all, I needed to keep fighting the urge to get
up and run home—my go-to response for most uncomfortable situations. My fight or flight response always seemed to be
on high alert. (Although it was usually in flight mode because
I'm quite a nice person and don't fight people.)

Despite the many excuses I had conjured up on my way
there, I hadn't cancelled the appointment which was a massive
step in the right direction. To be honest, I did try calling Ger
from my car, but couldn't get my Bluetooth thing to work. (I
could never get my bloody Bluetooth thing to work!)
What if I get a flat tire and can't reach Ger?
What if I get stuck in road construction and miss my appointment?
What if I can't find a parking space?
What if...?

"I'm sorry, can you repeat that?" I said in my confident professional sounding voice previously known as my phone voice
until technology made talking to people almost redundant. I
love technology. (Except for the Bluetooth thing in my car—
that's a piece of crap!)
She smiled again and said, "What brought you here today?"

Okay, time to let it all out on the table, so she can fix me up and send me on my way with a smile on my face and a skip in my step.

Taking a deep breath, I began. I explained how I'd suffered from anxiety most of my life and how I thought I'd managed it reasonably well until now (if 'managing it' meant hiding it away from everyone.) I thought the appointment was going fairly well until my body started to betray me.

No, don't you dare cry!

My mouth was dry, and I felt the horrible lump in my throat that wouldn't go away no matter how hard—or how many times—I tried to swallow it. My face felt like it was on fire as I fought so bloody hard to hold back the torrent of tears that threatened to spill.

Hold on, don't do the ugly cry, please don't do that!

I desperately wanted to run out of the room before I fell apart completely. Revealing my true self, was not something I wanted to share with a stranger, no matter how many letters she had behind her name. I looked towards the closed door thinking I might have time to escape, but it was too late. My body had already crossed over to the dark side and had descended into the emotional abyss of wet heaving sobs.

I cried buckets of tears that came from places I didn't know existed. Feeling like I'd already thrown my self-respect and dignity out the window, there wasn't much point in holding back now. I kept talking and crying until there was nothing left. I wanted to be honest, and there's nothing more honest than a woman sitting on a sofa with tears streaming down her face, makeup in places it should never be, and a growing pile of damp tissues on her lap.

What a bloody mess!

I was embarrassed and ashamed for losing control of my emotions and slowly raised my head to look at her. She was still smiling, but it looked like the smile you give to someone when you have no idea what the hell is going on.

"This is a safe place, Alicya. Please continue," she said, pronouncing my name slightly different from the first time, but still not quite nailing it.

Despite her reassuring words, something didn't feel right. Something was slightly off, but I held myself together enough to continue. I described how I felt over the past few weeks and how it had scared me so badly I'd thought I'd finally gone down the rabbit hole for good. I told her how I'd spent days crying for no apparent reason, and how I couldn't find the energy or the motivation to get out of bed, let alone the house.

I explained how my anxiety was so severe at times it was overwhelming and terrifying. It felt as though I'd spent my whole life battling it and it was now literally kicking my ass. I was mentally, emotionally, and physically exhausted. The dam had burst, and everything I'd carefully hidden away all these years spilled out before her. I had nothing left.

Well, this is embarrassing.

I reached for another handful of tissues and dabbed at my eyes and nose hoping I didn't look as disgusting as I felt. Slowly, I raised my head and waited for her to tell me she had all the answers. I waited for her to say, 'Don't worry, we can fix this, I know exactly what to do!' But instead, there was silence.

Finally, after what seemed like eternity, she smiled and said, "I understand. Is there anything else that's bothering you?"

Wait. What?

Anything else that's bothering me?
What. The. Hell.
Hadn't I just poured out all my thoughts and feelings for the last hour?
Hadn't I just cracked open in front of you?
Wasn't everything I had, already laying at your feet?
"No, that's it," I said, grabbing the damp tissues on my lap. I quickly dabbed at my eyes again, hoping my new waterproof mascara was holding up to its end of the bargain ($5.99 on sale at the local drugstore.)

It was the look on her face that gave her away. There was something in her eyes. It wasn't the look of when one wounded soul recognizes another because I knew that look well. No, this wasn't a look of connection at all.

It was a look of... pity.

Ugh pity, the lowest look of them all!

At that moment, I knew she couldn't possibly understand. I could tell from her expression she didn't have a clue how it felt to be in my skin, let alone in my head. It wasn't her fault, of course, it wasn't as if she was judging me. She was doing her job and holding space for me or whatever it is they call it. She was trying to be supportive. She was all smiley and nice, but I didn't want nice. I didn't even want supportive.

I wanted more. Much more.

What I wanted, what I desperately needed, were answers, solutions, a plan, a treasure map, a skeleton key... Something.

Anything but pity!

Not every therapist has personal experience with anxiety or depression, so maybe I was expecting too much. I wanted her to know exactly what it felt like. To have experienced it.

Perhaps I was reading her wrong, but I was disappointed. I suppose I expected more. Much more than just a smile.

"Shall we schedule your next appointment?" she asked, interrupting the commentary that was running rampant through my head. Apparently, my time was up.

"Thanks, you've been very helpful, but I'll have to think about it," I said as politely as possible. I quickly got up off the sofa, opened the door and left the office. I walked down the hallway and forced myself to smile as I passed the receptionist (although I'm sure it looked more like a grimace.)

Almost there. Almost there.

I rushed out the door, past the elevator, and down the stairwell. When I reached the street, I took a big deep breath of fresh air. It felt like I'd been holding my breath for hours. I kept walking and didn't look back until I was locked in the safety of my car.

I wish I could say I made another appointment with her and tried again. I wish I could tell you I saw another therapist or that I kept trying—but it would be a lie. I didn't do any of that.

I'm not sure what happened that day I left the therapist's office, but something inside of me changed. I don't know what it was exactly, other than I knew I was tired.

Tired of dealing with the constant worry, the panic attacks, and the anxiety. I was tired of pretending that everything was okay when everything was definitely not okay. I was tired of feeling less than normal. Tired of faking it.

I suppose I was just plain tired of everything!

What I did know was nothing was going to change unless I did something about it. I needed to make an effort to change myself, but effort sounded hard. The truth is I'm not a fan of doing hard things. I'd prefer to make a cup of tea, grab a good book and burrow down with the slight hope everything would be better tomorrow.

I wanted to take responsibility for my own well being and take charge of my own life. I was disappointed that I had allowed myself to reach this point and had let things get this bad. I had always led others to believe I could do anything. I was the first-born child. The leader. I had always been in control.

Just ask my sister.

When we were children, our parents apparently believed in child labour because I was babysitting from the time I was four years old. (Okay, maybe not four and my mum will say 'That never happened Alicya stop telling fibs!' But who are you going to believe—me or my child labour loving parents?)

From a young age, I was rarely allowed out of the house unless I took my younger sister with me. I swear I was the only kid in our neighbourhood who had to drag her little sister around everywhere.

There was no such thing as overprotective parents in those days. We all looked out for each other and if I wanted to play with my friends—dragging my sister around was the price I had to pay.

My sister may have sensed early on; she wasn't exactly a welcome addition to my social life. Thankfully, she was smart enough to keep quiet most of the time. So quiet in fact that I often forgot she was there. There were many times when I skipped home at dusk, not realizing I'd forgotten her and had to run back to where we had been playing to find her. I believed showing up at our house for supper without her would have put me on strict lockdown. There was no way in hell I was going to take that risk.

If you do ask my sister about my leadership qualities, she'll probably show you some of her childhood scars. Both physical and psychological. She may even tell you I didn't always lead safely or cautiously.

In my defence, I always told her not to follow me before things went horribly wrong. I take no responsibility (okay maybe a little responsibility) for her getting run over by our neighbour's car. Or when she fell off a water tank and broke her arm. Or even when she was dragged behind a train for half a mile before we were spotted by the police (admittedly, not the first and only time we were escorted home in the back of a police car.)

On second thoughts, don't ask my sister!

The point I'm trying to make is that as a young child, I was fearless. I was Huckleberry Finn (the girl version obviously). I climbed trees, built forts and treehouses, planned treasure hunts, and went on adventures.

When did everything start to change?

When did I start to lose myself?

The recent trip to the therapist's office had convinced me of one thing—I didn't want conventional therapy. I didn't want to talk about what I was thinking or feeling or rehash the events from my past.

It also made me realize I was no longer willing to accept my life as it was. I didn't like how I was living. I felt broken, and I needed to be the one to fix it. I wasn't exactly sure what I was going to do. Or know how I was going to go about finding out what that thing was—but I felt ready and determined to do something. Anything.

I knew I was falling. I had to believe I could save myself.

Overthinking was exhausting, and I was tired. So bloody tired. It had become almost impossible to turn off the constant barrage of thoughts, and restful sleep was now a distant memory. I was sliding downhill. I needed to rescue myself before it was too late.

I had often read that battling anxiety every day was a brave thing to do, but I don't think it has anything to do with bravery. For me, it's about holding on for dear life and doing what you need to do at that moment to get through.

It's about surviving.

I was tired of barely holding on. Tired of riding it out until the next wave came along. I didn't want to keep trying to survive, I wanted to thrive.

I was tired of the darkness.

I wanted my time in the sun.

That fearless young adventurer had gone somewhere, and I needed to find her. This exhausted and worn out version of that little girl needed to get ready to go on her biggest adventure. I needed to be fearless and find the courage and the energy to fight for myself.

There was no plan.

All I had was will and determination.

I just hoped it would be enough.

3. The Awareness Trifecta

There comes a time when a cup of tea and a little downward dog just doesn't cut it anymore.

When I was sixteen, a friend gave me a little blue pill (it could have been white, my memory of that night is a little hazy for obvious reasons.)

"It will help you relax," he said.

My family and I had recently moved from Wales to a small town in northern Canada, and I was anxious to fit in with my new group of friends. I was the 'new girl,' and I didn't quite know how to handle it.

We were standing in the kitchen drinking beer at a house party, and everyone seemed so relaxed. So comfortable in their own skin and I wanted that. Drugs were not usually my thing, but I took the pill and spent the rest of the night sitting on the floor in the corner of the living room unable to close my eyes.

I had taken that pill to relax, but my brain hadn't received that message. It had decided that it was going to fight it with all its might and if that meant keeping me up the entire night, unable to blink—so be it.

Drugs scared me.

Loss of control scared me.

Addictions scared me.

I didn't shy away from the occasional 'special brownie' or 'mushroom,' but I was afraid of becoming dependent and addicted. I didn't even smoke cigarettes.

When I was nine, I put a lot of effort into becoming a smoker like the older neighbourhood kids. I bought packs of menthols at the local corner shop, telling the shopkeeper they were for my mother, so they could just add it to our account. My mother never checked it, so I got away with it for a while. Fortunately, I was a terrible smoker. I couldn't inhale and coughed my lungs into my hands every time I took a puff. I was also too stupid to hide my pack of smokes properly and hid them under the coal bucket which sat next to our back door. Weirdly, my parents didn't believe me when I told them I was keeping them safe for a friend, so my smoking days were numbered.

Dependence on medication was something I feared, so it was an easy decision that it would be my last resort. Medication would be off the menu until I had completely exhausted all other options.

I needed an alternate plan.

Of course—as with most decisions I make in my life—I didn't quite think it through. I had no idea what I was going to do or where I was going to start.

Making myself a cup of tea (a great way to start anything worthwhile) I sat at the kitchen table and opened my laptop. The first thing I needed to do was research, so I turned to my old friend, *Google*. But it didn't take long to realize this may have been my first mistake. Entering 'anxiety,' into an internet search engine gave over 240,000,000 results.

Not to worry. I just need to narrow this down a little bit.

After several hours of reading umpteen articles and disappearing into numerous soul-sucking websites, my enthusiasm was beginning to fade. It was clear I needed to come up with a new plan quickly before my motivation dwindled into another cup of tea, a handful of chocolate biscuits, and a Netflix binge. Again.

I needed to be more selective in my search for answers.

Most of what I read advised anxiety sufferers to get professional treatment, and although I knew this was sound advice, it wasn't exactly what I was looking for. There were endless articles on what to do when suffering from anxiety. Drink chamomile or green tea. Take herbal supplements. Get a good night's sleep. Use essential oils. Exercise more. Take up yoga and learn to meditate.

These were all very helpful for other people I'm sure, but not for me. What I was specifically looking for was how to prevent anxiety from showing up in the first place.

Was that even possible?

I wanted to discover the cause of my anxiety and stop it before it rendered me useless. I didn't think a cup of chamomile and some downward dog was going to cut it.

Every time I felt defeated and ready to give up, I thought about that fearless little girl inside.

She wouldn't have given up so quickly.

She was tenacious.

She was a complete pain in the ass but, I needed to keep searching for her sake.

I read every psychology article on anxiety I could lay my hands on. Many of them said the same thing—you can manage anxiety with medication and Cognitive Behavioural Therapy (CBT). I knew lots of people who had bad experiences with anti-anxiety medication, and I didn't want to flatline emotionally. I didn't want to not feel the highs just because I hated feeling the lows. No, medication was not an option for me just yet, especially with my need for control issue.

The CBT route seemed like a better fit, but it meant regular visits with psychologists. That was not appealing to me at all. I needed to keep looking.

The problem with reading so much information was that it was easy to get bogged down with all the science. This area wasn't somewhere I was comfortable with. Science was like math. It dealt with absolutes. Black and white, and yes and no. I was more of a grey area kind of girl who barely squeaked by in math class. Dropped science as soon as possible and replaced it with English literature and drama classes. I was the head in the clouds, the daydreamer, the fidget. The girl with her head in a book (as long as that book had nothing to do with math or science.) I was the girl the French teacher threw her blackboard eraser at when I was staring out the window instead of conjugating French verbs—and just like that girl in French class—I found myself staring out the window once again.

Reading about the psychology of the brain was fascinating, but I'd read so much on this subject my head was full. I was informed, but I still wasn't any closer to finding what I was looking for. I didn't think I could absorb another number, statistic, result, study or any more data. I needed something else.

Meditation kept popping up as being effective in the management and prevention of anxiety, but everything I knew about meditation could fit on a Post-It note. I had meditated once or twice in the odd yoga class but in all honesty—it consisted of nothing more than closing my eyes and waiting until the instructor said to open them. I'm pretty sure that didn't count as meditation.

My most recent experience was when I forced myself to participate in going on a women's weekend retreat. I had signed up for it when I was feeling bored and had paid a non-refundable fee. This meant I couldn't back out without losing a shit load of money. (The lesson here is to never sign up for anything that's non-refundable, or when you're bored, or when your credit card is within arms reach.)

The retreat had been a huge leap out of my comfort zone especially since I had to share a room with two strangers. (Fortunately for me, they were very nice people and not homicidal or anything like that.)

During one of the yoga sessions, we were asked to chant while meditating where I quickly discovered that I am not what you'd call a natural chanter.

Is 'chanter' even a word? Sounds weird.

We also meditated while counting mala beads which I found quite strange because I kept forgetting where I was and had to start all over again. This seemed counterproductive. We even tried meditating like 'warrior women,' but I quickly discovered that if being a warrior woman meant I had to make strange noises while belly breathing—I was definitely going to let my fellow warriors down.

Sorry ladies.

One of the biggest issues I had with meditation was the sitting. Especially the cross-legged on the floor thing. All I could think about was how uncomfortable I was, while my hips, thighs, and lower back screamed at me to stop the madness. I tried not to fidget, but do you know what happens when you try really hard not to fidget? You fidget.

Opening one eye slowly, I peeked around the room to see if anyone else was struggling, but I got nothing. These women gave me nothing.

Nothing.

I saw no 'I'm hurting too, get me the hell out of here' looks or sly adjustments to let me know I wasn't alone in my pain.

It quickly became very evident that these women were not my women.

There was one thing I was good at—Savasana. I was quite good at laying down, so naturally, I loved Savasana (also known as the corpse pose in yoga to those that have no idea what the hell I'm talking about.) It was by far my favourite because I could do the corpse pose without any difficulty what so ever. I would have been happy to stay in that position all day—meditating and stuff—but after five minutes the instructor told us to get up and leave. Which I think was quite rude if I'm honest.

If meditation is as good as everyone says it is, then it was clear I needed to learn how to meditate correctly. The thought of quietly sitting alone with my thoughts was quite terrifying. I felt borderline insane on a regular basis. Just the thought of being alone in my own head was not something I looked forward to on the best of days. But if I was to do this, I needed to go all in. So that's exactly what I did.

I went all in.

Turning to my friend Google, I found plenty of local classes I could attend, but my social anxiety talked me out of it. Anxiety is quite good like that. It can talk you out of a wide array of social situations. Thankfully there were lots of courses available online. (The internet truly is an introverts best friend.)

Choosing the right kind of meditation was difficult. There was so much to consider, but the more I thought about it, the more I realized that I wouldn't be satisfied with merely learning to meditate. No, I needed to take it much, much further.

I needed to become a certified meditation instructor!

That's how my brain works. It goes from zero to one hundred in one ginormous leap. I rationalized (the fancy word I use for having a long conversation with myself) that if I paid to do a course that gave me something tangible in return—like a certificate—I would do everything I could to get my money's worth. It sounded like a perfectly logical plan to me.

Three hours later I found myself enrolled in a course that didn't cost a fortune and seemed well structured with great reviews. I eagerly signed up before I could change my mind.

This decision changed everything.

As I started to delve into the coursework, it became abundantly clear that what I lacked the most was awareness. Not awareness about the world, or the goings on of others (I was the self-appointed neighbourhood watch because I work from home with a good view of the street.)

No, what I lacked was *self-awareness.*

This came as a complete surprise to me because I thought I knew myself pretty well. I knew I was compassionate, kind, loyal, utterly self-absorbed at times, dramatic, a lousy cook, prone to avoiding housework, a lover of books, empathetic, introverted, anxious, occasionally depressed, a chronic worrier, a Scorpio, a raving lunatic... But what I thought was self-awareness—was not awareness at all. All I was doing was labelling myself. I needed to learn more about this *self-awareness* thing and find out how I could get myself some of it.

The last time I went looking for some sort of self-awareness was the time I went on the woman's retreat. We stood in a circle around a blazing fire in the garden, trying to avoid the thick choking smoke which always seemed to find you no matter how many times you moved away from it.

Earlier in the day, we were asked to write on a piece of paper something that we believed had been holding us back. The point of the exercise was to throw your paper into the flames to burn your troubles away and release them into the universe (or something like that.) The problem was I couldn't come up with one thing. The more I thought about what I should write, the more frustrated I became, so when it came to my turn, I just scribbled on the paper, folded it up tightly, and quickly threw it into the flames. I watched as the paper burned and changed colour. A slight breeze soon had the small black slivers of paper dancing and floating in the air sending my scribbles out into the universe. I feel sort of weird about that now.

I knew meditation wasn't going to solve all my issues because that would be asking too much, but I did start to feel more aware of how I thought and felt about everything. I even learned how to sit without fidgeting, which I thought was a huge accomplishment in itself.

While I continued my daily meditation practice, I also kept researching everything I could find on anxiety. What I realized was that there was something critical missing from all the endless articles and books I was reading. It was missing real people. People with real problems, who found real solutions.

I was tired of reading the same thing over and over again. I needed to find actual cases of how people overcame their depression and anxiety, in a way that connected with me.

That's when I discovered a woman named Byron Katie. She had battled severe depression, anxiety, and suicidal thoughts for many years and had found her own way through to the other side. She was sharing her process called *The Work,* and I connected with everything she was saying. I wanted to be like her. I wanted to find my own way through, and she gave me hope that I could do that. If Byron Katie could do it, I saw no reason why I couldn't do it too. (I find having an active imagination can sometimes replace my lack of self-confidence.)

I tried to embrace *The Work,* but during anxious times it seemed a bit complicated, and I got lost in the process. What she was saying made sense to me in theory, but it didn't seem simple enough at times when I needed it the most. I wanted to find an easier way to make it work for me. It needed to be so damn simple I could easily incorporate it into my daily life.

Simple. I liked simple.

All the research I had done boiled down to one concept—if I had any hope to control my worry and anxiety—I first needed to become aware of how I got to those states in the first place.

It all starts with awareness.

Awareness of my inner self.

Awareness of my thoughts, emotions, and actions.

All I needed now was to figure out how!

I knew that thoughts create emotions, and emotions made us behave the way we do. So, if I wanted to stop turning into a quivering idiot every time I felt anxious, then I needed to find out what thoughts were creating that feeling.

Slowing down and breaking everything down into manageable chunks was going to be vital because trying to digest everything at once would only lead to overwhelm and then that would be the end of that. I needed to simplify it in a way that made sense to me.

I looked at sorting out what was going on in my head like sorting out my overstuffed disorganized clothes closet. When my closet was overflowing and a complete mess, I couldn't function in there properly. I needed to organize all the crap going on in my head the same way. I was going to need boxes.

Putting everything into boxes helped sort all the good stuff from all the bad and unnecessary stuff. I needed to become more aware of emotions, thoughts, and actions, so taking out a pen and a notebook, I drew three boxes.

I labelled them THOUGHTS, EMOTIONS, and ACTIONS and called it—THE AWARENESS TRIFECTA. Mainly because there were three things to be aware of but mostly because it sounded cool. (Nerd alert?)

I had never given much thought to my thoughts or feelings, other than it was often something that made me run for cover and hide away from the rest of the world. Spending time examining my thoughts and feelings sounded a bit daunting, and if I am honest it was a whole lot of scary. I also believed it would only lead to more thinking and I did enough of that already. I certainly didn't believe I was capable of changing or controlling how I felt.

I thought I was—who I was.

I believed that the way people thought was part of their identity. I wasn't sure if I could, or even that I should try and change that. Was I ready?

Taming Crazy

4. Emotions and All the Feels

I found it. It was there all along,
I just didn't know what I was looking for.

The thought of exploring emotions was a little scary. Honestly, it was a fat load of scary.

I had been hiding from certain emotions for most of my life. Pushing them deep inside and refusing to let them see the light of day, or completely ignoring them because I didn't want to feel 'all the feels.'

Oh, sure I loved feeling the warm, fuzzy, comfortable ones, and the giddy joyful ones. I wanted to feel happy, excited and loved. I just didn't want to feel the ones that cut deep and hurt. Burying them meant I didn't have to face them and that sounded pretty good to me. I thought I could hide or ignore them forever, but now I realize they were always there—bubbling just below the surface—waiting for the right time to show up. Surprise!

Like many of us, I had grown up in an environment where being *too emotional* was frowned upon. It wasn't a written rule (at least I didn't think it was), but it was certainly implied. 'Suck it up,' 'Stop crying,' and the ever so popular 'I'll give you something to cry about' were familiar words we grew up with.

Showing certain emotions made you look weak and branded you a *crybaby*. It was much easier for everyone involved if children learned to bottle up all their emotional shit and push it deep down inside.

The deeper, the better.

Perhaps parents hung on to the faint hope that their kid would be able to pay for their own therapy by the time those deep-rooted emotions eventually came flooding to the surface.

I chose the 'never let them see you sweat' attitude quite early on. All I knew about emotions was that they hurt—and since I've never been a big fan of pain—I became very good at hiding what I was really feeling. I could be overly sensitive (if there is such a thing) and sad situations—real or imaginary—affected me deeply.

Delving into my suppressed emotions was not something I was looking forward to. I had spent most of my life building up a lovely big protective wall, but if I was to find that fearless little girl again, I was going to have to find a way to tear it all down. Hopefully, without getting buried in the rubble.

Most of what I read on the subject said you shouldn't be afraid to feel an emotion, but if I didn't exactly know what an emotion was, then how could I be okay with feeling it?

What I needed was a clear and straightforward definition of what an emotion was so that I could make sense of it. I turned to the internet for guidance, but the online dictionary didn't make it any clearer:

e·mo·tion — noun

a natural instinctive state of mind deriving from one's circumstances, mood, or relationships with others. *"she was attempting to control her emotions."*

synonyms: feeling, sentiment; More instinctive or intuitive feeling as distinguished from reasoning or knowledge.

"She was attempting to control her emotions." What the hell did that actually mean?

Diving back into the research I read that emotions gave off vibrational frequencies. This sounded all a bit too *new age-y* for me, but could it be that simple?

Were emotions just vibrations in the body?

If I was to believe this simple explanation, it meant that emotions were not something to be feared. If this was true, I needed to take this theory a little further so I could use it in a way that made sense to me. I had always looked at emotions as something negative. They had always seemed more like a big dark cloud hanging over my head than a vibration. Perhaps I had never looked at them up close, so I never saw them for what they were. I was afraid to feel them fully because the negative ones made me uncomfortable. I wanted to feel content and happy, but worry, self-doubt, and anxiety always seemed to elbow their way in.

What if instead of running away from them, ignoring them, pushing them aside, or covering them in chocolate, I paid attention to them instead?

What if I looked at every emotion as a building block with its own vibration?

Looking at each emotion as a separate entity like a building block, enabled me to see them differently. Some emotions were small and insignificant. They were easy to push aside, or to cover up and hide. While others—depending on the day or situation—were large, heavy, and impossible to ignore. There were days when several emotions piled up and become harder and harder to cover up. The worry block alone could sideline me for hours, if not days.

It became clear that because I wasn't dealing with any of these emotions when they first appeared, they would start to stack up. Slowly, this wall of emotional blocks became so high that I felt trapped, claustrophobic, and defeated.

I had always tried to ignore negative, scary emotions. Perhaps I thought it was the brave thing to do, but years of forcing them aside and pushing my way through them had the opposite effect of what I had hoped. Those emotional blocks were steadfast and solid, and over the years they had formed a strong foundation.

There were times when fear, self-doubt, and worry had shown up right after the other. I wasn't self-aware, so I didn't recognize them. I had allowed them to pile up on top of each other. Higher and higher they grew until it became difficult to breathe behind that wall. Eventually, everything had collapsed on top of me. I was left standing in the middle of the rubble waving a white flag that no one could see—desperately trying to surrender.

I thought the easiest solution would be to learn how to blast my way through the wall. I've never been a logical thinker by any stretch of the imagination, but it seemed perfectly reasonable to me.

However, I soon realized that blasting through them would only displace them. It would give a moment of reprieve, but it didn't remove them. Knocking them down gave me a false sense of safety. It gave me time to breathe, but the emotional blocks were still there. They were lingering, planning, and waiting for the moment when my defences were down so they can start rebuilding. Before I knew it, the hole in the wall had filled in again, and I was back to where I started. Behind that wall.

I needed a better solution. I had to look at emotions in a completely different way and change the way I thought about them. Instead of looking at them as harmful, I had to believe they were useful signals. They were helping me. Emotions were vibrations in my body that my brain sent out to alert me. They were telling me to pay attention.

They were my very own personal alarm system!

I needed to pay attention to my body. Not to all the aches and pains, but to all the vibrations I had been ignoring all these years. I needed to work on being fully aware of my body and get familiar with how it reacted to different emotions.

One morning, I was getting ready to go to a meeting. I don't remember where I was going or who I was meeting, but that's entirely irrelevant to the story anyway. As I stood in my closet looking for something to wear, I felt the familiar knot in the pit of my stomach. This was something I usually ignored—but not this time. Instead of trying not to feel it or pushing it away, I stayed aware of it and wrote it down in my notebook. The gnawing feeling grew in intensity, and soon my stomach started to churn.

As I continued to get ready, I felt my heart thumping in my chest, and my mind began to race. It was a horrible yet very familiar feeling.

You're going to be okay. Just breathe!
Intellectually, I knew this was my process. It was how my body reacted to specific situations, and as I continued to get ready, I wrote down everything I noticed. The palms of my hands felt a little clammy, and along with the churning, the thumping, and the sweating, my pulse was racing. It was evident that anxiety was setting in.

After managing to get through the meeting without embarrassing myself, I couldn't wait to get home and look at my notes from the morning's experience. I had witnessed my body's vibrations as if watching a movie. I had observed the process of how my body received the first sign—the gnawing sensation in the pit of my stomach. I had been entirely present and aware as more signs appeared, and because I didn't know how to deal with them—they had piled up. This was the proof I needed that showed there was a clear and definite process to my anxiety.

What would happen if I hadn't ignored the first sign?
What would happen if I learned how to deal with the first vibration?

I knew I wasn't the only one this was happening to because that would make me an anomaly and despite my self-importance—I wasn't that special. Perhaps everyone had their own set of vibrations which gave them different results. I had often read about the body and mind connection but had never fully understood it—until now. There was definitely a connection between emotions and the body's response. I had witnessed my process firsthand, and it was enlightening.

I had always tried to ignore uncomfortable emotions, but no matter how hard I worked to push them away, they persevered, and all those vibrations had piled up and taken their toll. That gnawing feeling in the pit of my stomach was always the first thing that reared its ugly head.

I hated that feeling.

When I think back to my teens, and well into my young adult years, it was often filled with anxiety. I remember suffering from blinding headaches, migraines and unexplained stomach aches all my life. Perhaps I was a slow learner, but it was starting to make perfect sense to me now. I guess I just needed to witness it for myself.

Asking someone who has suffered from anxiety or constant worry to just sit with it and feel it, isn't easy. It often results in forced smiles and vigorous eye rolling. (On occasion, it may even elicit a mild death threat.)

Facing emotions head-on can be so uncomfortable and frightening that we've become quite proficient with self-medicating. We eat, drink, smoke, and pop pills at an alarming rate. Not only to dull the pain but perhaps we do it in the hope it will miraculously turn us into who we want to be—instead of who we are.

"Alcohol makes me feel like I can do anything." My sister said when I asked her about it.

"Really?"

"Yep. It gives me confidence. Isn't that why we all drink when we socialize?"

"I suppose," I said. "But drinking doesn't do that for me. It just makes me tired, and I don't like the loss of control."

"That's because you're a control freak and most of us are not," she laughed.

"Rude."

As a teenager in a new town, in a new country, I had always felt like I didn't belong. To fit in, I did what everyone else seemed to be doing—I drank. This usually had one of two outcomes: a) Doing something I'd later regret, or b) Falling asleep in the back seat of someone's car. (It was the eighties, and cars had very roomy backseats for all kinds of activities.)

As my anxiety grew, the thought of drinking and not being in complete control scared the life out of me. (I will still drink wine at dinner but since I don't want to be found face down on my plate snorkelling spaghetti—I usually stick to one glass.)

I'm more of what you'd call a *feed your feelings* kind of girl. I eat to bury my emotions. I don't have to feel all the feels if I'm busy stuffing junk food down my throat. Hoping that the popcorn, chocolate, and chips will be enough of a buffer between me and the emotions I don't want to feel. I hadn't realized this was my pattern of behaviour until I started to pay attention. How's that for lack of self-awareness!

Worry, fear, anxiety, and depression were like an invisible fog. They crept silently under doorways and seeped through all the cracks, getting stronger and stronger by the minute. I couldn't see them, but I knew they were there. I waited, hoping if I ignored them long enough they would slink away quietly and disappear. They never did.

Now it was time to confront them.

I was so used to ignoring the signs I didn't realize they always knocked on the door to announce their arrival. I just never opened the door. They'd learned to be persistent. My ignorance meant I only acknowledged them when they were securely inside, but by then it was too late.

Many negative emotions are like that. They hate being ignored and will always find their way in.

Negative emotions are assholes!

When I was a kid, my mum and I would hide behind the sofa when the doorbell rang so that she didn't have to answer the door. She always told me it was because she didn't have time to talk to the salesmen—or the neighbour—or whoever it was behind that door. I think it's quite possible she had her own problem with anxiety. Although, it's probably best not to wade into mother issues right now. I have enough of my own.

'OMG!!!' I messaged my sister, knowing full well she'd be pissed at me for sending a message like that.

'WHAT???' She replied.

I started vigorously typing into my phone, but the damn autocorrect feature on my so-called smartphone was obviously deranged. My message only had a vague resemblance to what I was trying to say so I deleted it and typed 'CHAT?'

Chatting with my sister had a routine of its own. Our chats required intense preparation beforehand. Put the kettle on. Go to the loo. Let the dogs in or out and back again. A freshly brewed cup of tea was a must, and if the time were right, we'd make something to eat. Sista: a salad or a sandwich. Me: cereal or toast (because I'm twelve.)

"What's going on?" she asked.

"I've had a revelation."

"Another one?"

"That's a bit rude Sista. Yes, another one. But this one makes complete sense." I said, hoping she felt at least a little bit guilty about her reaction.

"Ok. Go on," she said, slurping her tea. "Shit, that's hot. I just burnt my lip."

I confess to feeling a slight tinge of satisfaction. *That'll teach her for not taking me seriously.*

"Mum taught me to hide from everything and not answer the door!" I blurted out.

"What does that even mean?"

I explained how mum had taught me to hide behind the sofa when the doorbell rang. Which in my mind, was the same as hiding from my emotions when they showed up. "She didn't do it intentionally of course, but it's a perfect analogy, isn't it?" I said, dipping my toast in my tea and taking a bite.

"That never happened, and if it did, where was I?"

"You were probably hiding behind the sofa too. You just don't remember. Anyway, it doesn't matter who was there, you're missing the point."

"Are you saying mum is the reason you're nuts?"

"Maybe."

This conversation wasn't going exactly the way I had planned it in my head. I thought she'd say I was on to something. I thought she'd be as excited as I was, but instead, she'd quickly let the wind out of my sails. She was seriously putting a damper on this conversation. She was bursting my fricken bubble, but I carried on anyway.

I told her I imagined emotions were like signals our bodies sent out. Like our own personal alarm system. Emotions were knocking on the door, and when we ignore them, they get more persistent.

"Mum never answered the door. She told me to hide from it and to wait it out, but wouldn't it have been easier to just answer the door, acknowledge who was there, and send them packing?" I said.

"Probably, but you both never answer the door."

"That's my point."

"Am I missing something here?"

"Bye Sista."

It was a Saturday morning, and Ger had been up for at least an hour before I made a bleary, eyed appearance. I poured myself a coffee and plonked myself on the sofa across from him.

"I'm going to answer the proverbial door from now on," I said, probably a little too loudly.

"Good morning," he replied, putting down his iPad. He was obviously surprised by my brilliance so early in the morning because there was no usual witty comeback.

"Proverbial. That's a big word for you first thing in the morning" he said.

Ah yes, there it was.

"I know, and it's probably not even the right word," I replied. Sipping my coffee and feeling the soothing liquid course through my body. There's nothing like a good strong cup of coffee in the morning. I prided myself on cutting back to one cup, but I wasn't fooling anyone. I just use a bigger mug now.

I told Ger about my latest discovery. About what I thought an emotion was and how I was going to deal with every emotion that showed up instead of ignoring it. I was going to answer the door from now on. We agreed it was probably best for everyone involved not to blame my mother.

"It does make sense in theory," he said.
"Really?"
"Yes, I think you're on the right track."
Damn, I love this man!

Despite my initial excitement, I was nervous about meeting my emotions head-on. I had no idea what kind of emotional baggage I might have to unpack. But I believed if I could learn to deal with the small stuff first, then I'd soon be slaying dragons. (Not actual dragons, of course. I'm Welsh, and we have quite an affinity for dragons.)

5. Slap A Label on Those Babies

"Worry does not empty tomorrow of its sorrow;
it empties today of its strength." ~ unknown

When I was nine years old, I developed a severe throat infection. Being allergic to penicillin and swallowing teaspoon after teaspoon of mentholated slime didn't help. And I ended up in hospital.

(Back in the 'no seatbelt' days, many of us were slathered with *Vick's* at the first sign of a cold, and some of us were forced to swallow it. Since parents didn't know it was toxic when ingested, the company added *vapour rub* in big letters to its label when they discovered that parents—just like mine— were lubricating their sick children's insides as well as their chest, throat, and feet with the stuff. Most of us survived if you were wondering.)

I was immediately put into quarantine and was scared to death. I had been to the hospital several times for various reasons but had never been left alone overnight there before. (I still may be a little bitter about this.) It could have been the fact I was all alone in that hospital room or that no one was allowed near me without looking like they were treating *E.T.*, but I truly believed I was going to die. Considering nobody had thought to explain to a frightened little girl what the hell was happening—I think my concern was valid.

One of the nurses—who for some unknown reason I secretly named Plummy—pointed to a chart hanging on the wall directly across from my bed. It had a smiley face on one end and a sad face on the other, and she asked me to point to the one that best described how I was feeling. She needed to know how much pain I was in, but even back then I couldn't help think there were only two options.

You're either happy, or you're sad.

The next step on my journey was to find out exactly what kind of emotions I was dealing with. I knew when I felt an emotion gnawing away in the pit of my stomach, but it wasn't going to help if I didn't know what the emotion was. In order to learn how to ultimately manage anxiety, I needed to know what emotions I had been ignoring or pushing away all these years and slap a label on them.

I wasn't always the happy smiley face on the hospital chart, but I wasn't the sad face either. Sadness was one emotion I rarely dealt with. Even when I suffered from bouts of depression, I wouldn't describe it as feeling sad. Frightened, worried, exhausted, isolated, mostly numb—but rarely sad.

There were plenty of other emotions that I often pushed away and ignored, and these were the ones I needed to explore. Grabbing my notebook, I wrote down all the negative and positive emotions I could think of:

NEGATIVE

Sad	Isolated	Angry	Bored
Disrespected	Depressed	Mad	Nervous
Frightened	Lonely	Frustrated	Stressed
Worried	Numb	Annoyed	Anxious
Overwhelmed	Exhausted	Heartbroken	Shame
Disappointed	Guilty	Scared	Chaotic

POSITIVE

Happy	Confident	Content	Pleased
Joyful	Loved	Excited	Delighted
Relieved	Proud	Grateful	Glad

It was much easier to come up with negative emotions than positive ones. Which I admit, was a bit disappointing.

Was disappointed on my list?

I often described my mood or emotion as being *pissed off*, but to be honest, I'm not sure what being *pissed off* meant. I had never stopped to think about what the core emotion was that I was feeling. It was much easier to say I was pissed off because then I didn't have to look too deeply into why I felt that way.

My latest experience with self-awareness clearly showed how my body exhibited anxiety before my meeting but the first sign—the gnawing in the pit of my stomach—wasn't anxiety at all. Anxiety had been the result.

So, if anxiety isn't the first emotion I experience, what is?
And if I deal with that emotion as soon as it shows up, could I prevent
the anxiety all together?

This concept was exciting. It was more exciting than the time I conquered my fear of heights by rappelling off a scarily high training tower. I say conquered, but it's more like I had made peace with the universe before throwing myself off the platform. (I had also cleaned out my underwear drawer in preparation for my impending death which may have helped.)

If I was on the right track, then it was safe to believe that anxiety was the result of ignoring all my other emotions. It could be worry, fear, frustration, or overwhelm that I felt first—and when I ignored it—it escalated into anxiety.

Worry was something I always battled. My brain kept me awake at night worrying about the stupidest things—little things, big things, ridiculous things. Usually, they were things I had no control over.

"Don't worry so much," Ger would say when he saw my furrowed brow. "It doesn't solve anything."

My dear darling husband, if only it were that easy. If only I could be just like you, without a care in the world. If only I could switch it on and off. What a wonderful world you must live in.

I never understood why he didn't worry about whether our boys had done their homework, eaten enough, slept enough, or worried about whatever *Dr. Phil* had told me to worry about. When our boys missed their curfew, I envisioned them in trouble, alone and scared. Ger didn't.

They probably wondered why I wasn't there to save them while their dad was too engrossed in a movie to care.

"See, I told you not to worry," Ger would say, as the boys burst through the front door half an hour late.

I believed my worrying had a role in keeping them safe. My worry wasn't hurting them, but it definitely took its toll on me. I thought sleepless nights was the price you pay for being a loving, caring parent.

According to the internet and the many books I read, too much anxiety and stress can kill you. It can increase your risk for obesity, heart disease, Alzheimer's disease, diabetes, depression, gastrointestinal problems, and even asthma.

Anxiety and stress are on the rise.

It's everywhere. But how do you avoid stress when it seems so unavoidable in today's multitasking, hustling, competitive, Instagrammed world?

What if stress is a result emotion like I think anxiety is?

What if it's become so socially acceptable to say we're stressed, we don't even think about all the other emotions that may have played a part in creating it?

What if *Mr. Frustrated* was knocking on the door while standing under an umbrella (obviously it's raining because otherwise, he would look stupid standing there under an umbrella!) What if a few minutes later, *Mr. Tired* and *Little Miss Overwhelm* showed up?

What if they're all frantically banging on the door and you refuse to answer it until *Mr. Big Ass Stress* shows up and kicks the door down with his size 14 *Dr. Martens*?

(If you do not see these emotions as the animated *Mr. Men* series then you missed out on an essential part of childhood.)

"I have no idea what you're talking about," said Ger, when I explained my *Mr. Men* analogy.

"Remember *Mr. Tickle*?" I asked, fully expecting him to remember, despite having completely different childhoods in different countries.

"I think we may be thinking of an entirely different thing right now," he said.

"Okay forget *Mr. Tickle*. What about *Mr. Happy*?" As soon as I said it, I knew I'd lost him. This wasn't going as well as I'd planned it in my head. I explained my new theory again—without the *Mr. Men* analogy.

"What if anxiety and stress is the result of ignoring all the other emotions that had come before it? Sort of like an emotional pileup."

"Okay. That makes sense," he said.

"Really?" I asked, surprised that he understood what I was saying. (Apparently, not everyone needs visualization like I do, which I think is just plain weird.)

"Yes, really," he said.

"I'm banishing stress and anxiety from my vocabulary," I announced quite proudly to my sister the next day.

"How can you banish anxiety if you suffer from anxiety. Isn't it a diagnosis? You can't just say you don't have anxiety anymore unless you've found some miracle cure, and Sista you're good, but not that good" she said.

There are days when I don't know why I talk to her. This was one of those days.

"True. But haven't you noticed that everyone seems to be anxious about something these days? We used to say we're thinking about something—or worried or concerned. Now we say we're anxious as if being 'worried' is beneath us. It's like having anxiety is cool—unless you actually have anxiety—then it's not so cool".

My sister and I are similar in many ways. So similar in fact our doctor had even mentioned it once. Let me explain.

Several years ago, my regular doctor had retired and because I was overdue for the dreaded pap smear (ugh) I needed to find another one. My sister suggested I visit hers and had discussed it with him in advance. (I like to think it was to explain to him how awesome I was, but it was probably more of a courtesy warning.)

During the appointment, the doctor could probably sense how nervous I was by the deathly grip I had on the sides of the table and the way my back immediately stuck to the paper cover. I placed my feet awkwardly in the stirrups, closed my eyes and tried to pretend I was somewhere else. Anywhere but there. To his credit, he attempted to calm my nerves by talking, but who can listen to someone blabbing away when they're 'down there' looking at your bits?

I kept my eyes closed tightly and waited for the nightmare to be over when I heard a voice from between my thighs, "I can tell you are sisters!" Realizing immediately what he had said and where he was positioned when he said it, he pushed his stool back just in time as my knees clamped shut like a bear trap. Thankfully his reflexes were good.

"I can tell you are sisters because you sound alike," he said. It was a valiant attempt at saving the moment, but the mood was broken, and it ended our relationship (with the doctor I mean, not my sister.) I was mortified, but my sister thought it was the funniest thing ever. She's not very supportive at times like these.

As I was saying, my sister and I are quite similar, but anxiety wasn't something she had personally dealt with. However, she had suffered from a great deal of stress for most of her adult life. I believed that if I could find a way to manage my anxiety and her stress—we'd be golden (like *Ponyboy golden*.)

"We need to pay attention to what we're actually feeling. We need to work on being more self-aware." I told Sista the next time we talked.

"Okay but I think I'm already pretty self-aware," she said.

"Trust me you're not. I thought I was too, but I was not even close."

I explained why we needed to try and identify the first emotion that shows up instead of ignoring it. How to feel it and recognize it.

"I'll try," she said.

"Try hard Sista," I replied as I hung up the phone.

Over the next few weeks, I became more and more aware of what my body was doing and how it reacted to emotions. The meditation practice was going well, and because the course required journaling to track my progress, it gave me a valid reason to write down everything I was feeling and thinking.

I discovered that when I felt the gnawing sensation in the pit of my stomach, it was usually because I was worried about something. It was a familiar feeling because I was always worrying about something. If worry were an Olympic event—I would have reached the podium every time—both Summer and Winter Olympics. Plus, I have dual citizenship so I could compete for two countries at the same time. I think that may be against the rules, but you get the point. I'm hardcore.

Worry was my base emotion.

Worry was my kryptonite!

Despite the fact I was a world-class worrier, I had never actually dealt with any of the worry. I usually ignored it because being told 'not to worry' was bloody annoying. I stuffed worry down deep inside and let the churning continue to gnaw away at my soul. (I warned you I was a bit dramatic.)

'Don't worry.'

'Stop worrying.'

'Think positively.'

I'd heard these words most of my adult life. I would respond by plastering a sweet smile on my face (or a grimace, we'll never really know) but despite the smile, I sometimes wanted to punch them in the face.

'If I could shut it off that easily don't you think I would?' I wanted to scream. I knew they were only trying to be helpful, but it doesn't help. It never helps.

Slapping a label on the gnawing sensation in the pit of my stomach made sense to me. That label was *worry*, and it was usually the first one knocking on the door. It was often followed by the rapid heartbeat and the racing pulse which I labelled *self-doubt* and *fear*. By the time anxiety forced its way in through the door dressed up like nausea, perspiration, and tears, it was too late.

Welcome to crazy!

6. Thoughts, All the Damn Thoughts

*"I've suffered a great many catastrophes in my life,
most of which never happened."* ~ Philip Twain

Feeling pleased with what I'd discovered so far, I decided
to ride the high and tackle what I knew would be the
toughest part of the *Awareness Trifecta*—my thoughts.

Putting my thoughts under the microscope was going to be
challenging. Overthinking was my downfall. If there was
something to think about you can bet I'd already thought
about it frontwards, backwards, upwards, downwards and everything in between. According to various studies I had read,
human beings can process between 50,000 and 80,000
thoughts per day. No wonder we're all so damn exhausted all
the time!

Most of these thoughts are in our sub-conscious mind and
never see the light of day but even so—that's a hell of a lot of
thoughts rattling around our heads every day.

The sub-conscious thoughts don't bother us too much.
They control our everyday motions and allow us to live our

lives. We don't need to consciously think about how to walk across the room, brush our teeth, or eat a family-size chocolate bar while binge watching our favourite shows—we just do it. Our brain creates a sort of pathway to bypass the conscious thinking part of doing repetitive actions. It's like our operating system running in the background, doing all the things we don't need to think about. It frees us up for more important things like worrying. Or wondering why there's never chocolate in the house when you need it. Or why you can never find the damn remote… or your keys… or your phone… or your glasses. (You get the point.)

Most of us who deal with anxiety, constant worry, self-doubt or low self-esteem are over thinkers.

It's who we are.

We can have one seemingly harmless thought. Which leads to hundreds of damaging, soul-sucking thoughts. Before we know it, we fall down the rabbit hole, land on our ass dazed and confused, wondering how the hell we got there.

"What are you thinking about?" I asked Ger, as he sat quietly on the sofa.

"Nothing," he'd reply.

"How is that even possible?"

"I don't know. It just is."

I never understood this. I just thought he just didn't want to share his thoughts with me. He had always been a private person, and I respected that, but I wanted to know what the hell he was thinking.

How can he not be thinking?

Every time I asked him, I always expected a different answer. I never received one.

When I first considered meditation, I didn't think there was any way it would work for me. How on earth could someone who thought as much as I did, be expected to sit there quietly and not think?

The very thought of being alone inside my own head for any length of time was daunting and a tad bit terrifying. I had even tried to talk myself out of it, but if I was to make any difference in my own life, I had to do something different. I had to do hard things. (Handing over my hard-earned cash for it was also a huge motivator.)

I was studying a type of meditation called Vipassana, more commonly known in the western world as mindfulness meditation. Vipassana means *insight* in Pali (the language of early Buddhism.) Of course, this didn't mean much to me at first because I didn't quite understand what *insight* meant.

Was I going to be able to look into the future? Intriguing, but highly unlikely.

Vipassana was often described as a way to see everything as it is. To look at things with no judgment or condemnation. To think without attaching to the thought.

Wait. What?

'Not attach to the thought?'

What the hell does that mean?

As I made my way through the course and read the book *Mindfulness in Plain English* by Bhante Gunaratana, it became apparent that I wasn't always fully aware of what I was thinking. My thoughts usually started off innocently enough, but quite often ended in a deep plunge off a very high cliff.

I had a lot to learn.

A significant factor in the way I thought was my obsessive-compulsive issues, which only served to ramp up the thought machine. I call it the 'BUT WHAT IF' factor and it made even the simplest of questions, almost impossible to answer.

'What is your favourite colour?'

I don't know. I can't possibly think of just one. Maybe purple, but not the lilac kind of purple, and I don't like it all the time, so I suppose the answer's not purple. Although dark purple is quite nice. Sometimes I like blue and some shades of green. Not bright green or... There used to be a rhyme 'blue and green should never be seen unless there's a colour in between.' That can't be true. I'd like to say my favourite colour is red, but it isn't. I always gravitate to black and grey clothing, and I drive a black vehicle, but I suppose that doesn't mean it's my favourite. I like to decorate our house with whites, blues, greens, earth tones but is white a colour? This is a stupid question. Pass.

Choosing just one answer, meant that I'd spend at least the next half an hour thinking of reasons why my answer would be wrong.

James Spader, the American actor, shared his struggle with obsessive-compulsive issues in a 2017 interview he did for *Build NYC*. He revealed that he found it incredibly difficult to answer questions in absolutes due to these issues.

James, I feel you. We should meet.

(Full disclosure: I possibly have an unhealthy obsession with Mr. Spader, and I'm sharing this fact with you because he won't see it. He won't see it... right?)

Anyway, he told a story of when he was interviewed by a reporter for a feature in *Rolling Stone magazine*, they call *The Last Word*. He was happy to oblige, but as soon as the interview began, he knew he was in trouble. Every question he was asked required a definitive answer. Questions, like 'What is your favourite book?' 'Who is your favourite director?' had his brain spinning and every question he tried to answer became a rambling story on why he couldn't pick a favourite. It didn't take long for his anxiety to escalate.

When it was decided that perhaps the interview wasn't such a great idea after all and maybe they should end it, he was so relieved he felt his anxiety level decrease almost instantly.

Obsessive-compulsive issues and the 'BUT WHAT IF' factor were two reasons I didn't think meditation would work for me. I obsess about everything. I couldn't see how I was going to sit still without going completely insane inside my own head, but gradually it became easier.

I did have days when it was difficult to sit because of the continuous chatter in my head but learned that this was perfectly normal. There was even a name for it, *monkey mind*. Even seasoned meditators—the ones that have been meditating for many years—have days when they deal with *monkey mind*. Knowing this made me feel a little better about myself.

Managing the days when there's a lot of chatter in your head is the whole point of meditation. *Who knew?*

The meditation practice was going well, but it was the time outside of it that needed the most work. Meditation is focused concentration, but the rest of the time my mind felt free to roam. Sometimes it wandered to the wrong part of town. It travelled down dark allies and into abandoned buildings. I needed to take more responsibility for where I allowed it to go. Supervising my thoughts twenty-four hours a day was impossible, but I could become more aware of when my mind was stepping into areas it shouldn't go.

It was free to wander hand-in-hand with creativity and imagination, but I needed to set up boundaries when it came to damaging thoughts. All those negative thoughts were creating havoc, and I was going to have to find a way to manage them if I had any hope of finding peace.

7. What the Hell Was That?

Thoughts can run rampant like a hatchet-wielding maniac on a murder-ous rampage; there's no warning or time to prepare.

I've always envisioned worst case scenarios.

It's not as if I made a conscious decision to think about the worst possible thing in the entire world. It just sort of happens. It was usually when I was busy minding my own business just living life as you do, and suddenly it would hit me right between the eyes with no warning.

There were times when I'd be driving somewhere, and while sitting at a red light at a busy intersection, I envisioned myself lifting my foot off the brake as my vehicle slowly rolled out in front of a semi-truck. Most of the time, the thought was only a spark. As brief as a blink of the eye. But there would be times when I could envision the impact. It was loud and startling. The air filled with the sounds of metal on metal, screeching tires, and blood-curdling screams, as shattered glass rained down. The light would turn green, and I continued my journey as though nothing had happened.

I couldn't imagine any *reasonably sane* person would think these thoughts, so I never told a soul about them. I carefully pushed them to the back of my mind, burying them as deeply as I could, and they stayed there, hidden away until the next time. There was always a next time.

These thoughts weren't the typical worrying kind of thoughts. They didn't seem to have a long-lasting effect or create anxiety. They were dark, strange, and violent. Occasionally seductive, and always dramatic. They were the thoughts that frightened me most of all because I felt they were proof that something was inherently wrong with me.

Sometimes these thoughts happened in the middle of the night as I laid in bed wide awake or when I was on the edge of falling asleep. The thoughts would almost always be very violent which was disturbing because I abhor violence. These thoughts would be like a vision. A real-life nightmare that would play over and over until I fell into an exhaustive sleep.

Waking up a few hours later, I'd feel more tired than when I went to bed. I tossed and turned most of the night, replaying the terrifying scene which never seemed to have an off switch. I'd wake up several times, but when I finally managed to fall back asleep, the replay would start again. From the beginning.

The same thoughts would still be replaying in my head when I woke the next morning. It was as if the thoughts had morphed into dreams and back into thoughts once again.

It terrified me.

They were like movies. Every scene would be carefully performed, and no matter how hard I tried, I could never seem to rewrite the script.

'I had a horrible dream again last night,' I told Ger the next day when he saw the worried look on my face.

'What about?' he would ask.

Sometimes I'd share parts of it with him, leaving out the most disturbing details for fear he'd see how insane I really was. He loved me unconditionally, I knew that, but he didn't know just how unsettling my thoughts were. I wasn't going to take the risk.

During my research, I discovered these thoughts I had been hiding all these years are called *intrusive thoughts*.

Imagine my joy in finding out that *intrusive thoughts* are quite common and surprisingly normal for someone suffering from anxiety and obsessive-compulsive issues. I was sort of normal in a totally fucked-up kind of way.

Many people experience *intrusive thoughts*, but they can let them go. Sure, they may think 'Where the hell did that come from?' But they don't dwell on it. I—on the other hand—would replay it over and over again all the while wondering if I was going insane.

Intrusive thoughts are harmless in most cases. They're only thoughts based on our very worst fears. Anxiety and obsessive thought patterns make them seem like they are so much more than that. They can get stuck in a continuous loop and letting them go, can seem like an impossible task.

One psychologist—who had just given birth to a healthy baby boy—found that she couldn't stand at the top of her stairs without imagining herself dropping her baby down them. She envisioned his tiny, helpless body writhing in pain.

She was experiencing *intrusive thoughts* but because she knew what they were—that they were based on her worst fear—they didn't concern her. Imagine that!

Intrusive thoughts can run through your head like a hatchet-wielding maniac on a murderous rampage. There's no warning or time to prepare.

They seem so real to us but knowing they're relatively common—that they're based on fears and not something you would ever act on—brings a sort of comfort that's hard to describe. It's almost as if just by naming the thought and calling it out instead of trying to bury it, takes away its power. There's no longer any guilt or shame surrounding it because you know they mean nothing.

It's like watching a scary movie with all the lights on while eating extra buttery popcorn. It's much less frightening than being alone in the dark, jumping at every strange noise, and hiding under your duvet. You're watching the same damn movie, but you know that's all it is. A movie.

(Spoiler Alert: In my movie, everyone survives, and they're all in the sequel.)

8. A Simple Plan

Keeping things simple is much harder than it seems.

With so many thoughts running through my head it was clear I needed to come up with a plan. I had foolishly believed I could keep all these thoughts clear in my head, but who was I kidding? Those damn thoughts were what got me here in the first place.

During meditation, it was much easier to see thoughts as singular because I had learned to see each thought as it entered and left my mind. (A bloody miracle in itself!) I didn't attach to it, analyze it, judge, or blame it (well, most of the time I didn't.) I merely observed it, and I loved that.

Vipassana meditation wasn't just the time spent meditating. It is a way of life. I had to fully embrace this if I had any hope of getting out from under the avalanche of thoughts that always morphed into something bigger and more damaging.

The point of Vipassana or mindfulness meditation is to take what you learn during your practice and apply it to everyday life. It was about being present as often as possible and not letting your mind wander into places that caused your own pain. I've never been a big fan of pain, so it was time to put it to the test.

I had grown to love my time spent in meditation. Ten, twenty, or thirty minutes a day of sitting in mental peace and quiet was something I looked forward to. It was clear I needed to use the same technique of being fully present and apply it to every other part of my life. At home, at work, or standing in the checkout aisle at the supermarket. (Not that I had spent a lot of time in a supermarket lately due to the whole social anxiety thing.)

Separating one thought from another without actively meditating was difficult. So difficult that I started carrying a little notebook around and wrote down any thought that was troubling me. 'Time to collect my thoughts' took on a whole new meaning because I quite literally had a place to collect them. Anytime I experienced a strong emotional reaction, I wrote down what I was thinking. There were times when it was frustrating, and I had to keep reminding myself I could do hard things. This was only research, and necessary for the greater good (or at least for my greater good.) I wasn't going to quit this now like I had done with everything else that I had found 'too hard.' This was far too important.

With practice, it became much easier to weed out the damaging thoughts from the garden-variety thoughts like *'Can I convince Ger that popcorn is a perfectly healthy replacement for supper two nights in a row?*

When my notebook wasn't within arm's reach (which meant I would need to get up off my ass), I used any piece of paper I could put my hands on. Usually, Post-It notes. They were plentiful in our home because the older I got, the more forgetful I seemed to be. Ger believes I have selective memory loss and only seem to forget things that aren't about me. I don't think he has concrete evidence of this though so I wouldn't take his word for it.

Within a matter of days of writing everything down, I noticed a shift. I felt lighter and seemed to have fewer troubling thoughts. I was more present outside of my meditation practice. Mentally—I was starting to feel better. I didn't want to get my hopes too high, but life was starting to feel *different*.

This *shift* was huge. I needed to share this with Ger as soon as possible, but as usual, he was at work (needing to work to pay the bills sure puts a damper on things.) I buried myself in my own work and waited.

After many years of marriage, I'd learned he was much more likely to listen to me if I didn't blast him with my issues as soon as he came through the front door. It was a practice in patience. I was like our dogs. Sitting on the step, tail wagging, waiting to be acknowledged. I do think I was a little better at this than the dogs, but I could be wrong.

"How was your day?" I asked Ger as soon as he stepped into the kitchen.

"Busy," he answered.

"Good busy or bad busy?" I asked, knowing his answer would determine my next move.

"Good busy."

Excellent!

I watched him climb the stairs to the bedroom and waited while he changed out of his work clothes. This was always an agonizingly slow process for some reason. I'm not sure what takes so long but waiting for Ger to change his clothes or get ready for anything seemed to take forever (or at least longer than I would like.)

"Do I seem different?" I asked when he finally joined me in the kitchen again.

"What do you mean 'different'?"

"I mean do I seem different lately? Calmer?"

"Yes, actually you do. I was going to mention it but didn't want to throw you off."

"Throw me off what?"

"You know how you get."

"What do you mean, 'How I get'?"

"You tend to obsess about everything, but right now you're more focused. I didn't want to say anything and spoil it."

Hmmm. Calmer. More focused.

I don't hear that very often. To be honest, I never hear it. I was clearly changing, and people were noticing. Okay, maybe only Ger was noticing, but I'll take what I can get.

9. Actions, Habits, And Quirks

The road is paved with good intentions.

With a good grasp on identifying thoughts, it was time to tackle the final part of the *Awareness Trifecta*... Actions. This was something I'd never thought about. I was more adept at spotting the actions and behaviours of other people. People-watching was an art form.

Most of my actions, habits, and quirks were harmless (or so I thought.) I definitely didn't think they affected other people, but the more I thought about it, the more I realized how annoying I could be. (I'm probably as shocked as you are by that revelation.)

When it came to actions—I was compulsive—ideas would show up bright, loud and impossible to ignore. My life had been filled with one fabulous idea after another and off I'd go, only to abandon it entirely when it didn't go my way. I started and never finished well-intentioned projects all the time. I created several blogs, took up photography, woodworking, cooking, knitting, quilting...

I left a trail of discarded attempts along the way, and they served as constant reminders that once again, I had failed to finish what I started.

It was clear that my emotions determined my actions. If I didn't *feel* like doing something, I'd make any excuse not to do it. I left piles of clothes on the closet floor and often *forgot* to clean out the bathroom sink after I used it (just one reason why Ger and I used separate bathrooms.) I left piles of books and notes everywhere. I was messy.

Procrastination was another lovely skill I possessed. It's an avoidance behaviour. A coping mechanism of putting off something that will possibly be uncomfortable or difficult.

Even the quirks I thought were endearing, were not all that endearing after all and as I began to take notice of my behaviours, I saw there were some definite patterns. Seeing them on full display was annoying (even for me), and I had to remind myself frequently that this was still the research stage. I was to observe and report—nothing more (which was actually much harder than it sounds.)

There were times when I'd catch myself doing something I wasn't happy about, like grabbing more chocolate out of the fridge when I'd already eaten more than I should. I noticed I always had an excuse why I couldn't exercise that day, or binge-watched *Netflix* when I had so many things I should have been doing. (*Netflix* is like eating a bag of chips. You always need 'just one more.')

Although my primary focus was to observe my own actions, I'll be honest and say that it was much more fun and incredibly easy to spot the behaviours of other people. (It's not creepy if it's for research, right?)

I started paying attention to the people around me. Not just what they said, but what they did, and soon discovered little behaviours I hadn't noticed before. Like how a co-worker's tone of voice changed dramatically when she was frustrated. How another chewed her fingernails when she was nervous. Another one always seemed to be complaining, gossiping or throwing her co-worker under the bus, the train, or whatever else she had at her disposal.

Knowing emotion was driving these behaviours was fascinating. I was witnessing *cause and effect* right before my eyes.

One of the surprising yet disappointing things I discovered was that my most frequent action—was inaction.

When I felt frustrated, overwhelmed, or when self-doubt paid a rather lengthy visit, it paralyzed me. I pushed my feelings aside—and no matter how hurt I was—I ignored it and did nothing about it.

The silent treatment was another of my go-to behaviours. I was quite good at shutting down and believed that not saying anything at all was probably my best move. I hated any kind of confrontation. Our house was deathly quiet when Ger and I didn't see eye to eye on something because he disliked arguments as much as I did, and was even better at the silent treatment than I was.

I could easily not talk to people for a very long time unless it was Ger. I almost always broke the silence first when it came to him. I sat across from him and stared while he was watching some mindless thing on the telly (or at least he pretended to.)

"What?" he would ask.

"I don't want to fight."

"I wasn't aware that we were."

You're being passive aggressive! I wanted to shout at him, but I held my tongue. "Well, whatever this is, I don't want to do it. Can we just stop the silent treatment?"

"I'm not giving you the silent treatment. It was you that walked off." He answered.

Oh, for fuck's sake. Let's try this again. "Ok, that's true. I'm sorry."

"I'm sorry too," he'd say.

And it was over just like that.

I'd read somewhere that couples who argue and fight have the best relationships, but I don't think that's true for everyone. People can say some shitty things when they're angry, and nothing good can come from hearing that. You can never take words back no matter how hard you try and since many of us can remember every hurtful thing said to us throughout our entire lives—silence is golden in my world!

I know some people who thrive on a good argument. They love the fight and can argue until the cows come home (I'm not a farmer and have no idea when the cows come home or even know where they would have been to make them want to come home, but I think it means a long time.)

Healthy discussions are great, but confrontations, arguments, fights—call them what you will—I avoid them at all costs. They make me incredibly uncomfortable, and when I'm feeling uncomfortable, I shut down. (How's that for self-awareness?)

Consistent behaviour over time can become a habit without realizing it. Some people slam doors when they're mad, snap at you when you ask a simple question, or make excuses for why they can't be there (guilty as charged.) Sometimes our actions are much subtler. Even a yes or no answer from someone who's usually quite chatty is an action, driven primarily by emotion.

We're complicated creatures (some of us are more complex than others as Ger likes to point out), but deep down we're all quite similar. Our actions and behaviours are driven by how we feel in that moment.

But could it be that simple?

The answer is… maybe.

Although destructive behaviours need to be explored to change them, some behaviours are quite harmless and help shape our personality (even if they may seem weird to others.) Not all behaviours need changing or exploring, and some habits we have are quite humorous (or annoying depending on how you think about them.)

People with obsessive-compulsive issues tend to have a wide spectrum of behaviours they frequently perform in order to function. They create behavioural habits to make sense of their world even if they make no sense to those around them.

One of my quirks involves Q-tips. If I see clean white Q-tips in a nice little container in your bathroom, I will leave with at least four of them neatly tucked away in my pocket. I can't explain it. It's a compulsive behaviour, and I don't even use them. They almost always end up in the washing machine because I never take them out of my pocket—so not only do I 'borrow' them—I also waste them. (My sincerest apologies to all my Q-tip victims out there. Although I'm pretty sure you don't know who you are!)

Not all behaviours can be easily explained. There are a lot of quirks and habits that defy explanation or have been so ingrained in our psyche, it's impossible to place where they came from. Even my husband, who is the most logical, well-balanced human I know, has some behaviours that defy explanation. They're not harmful. Some may think they're endearing, but I find them just plain weird. Here's just one example;

Ger is a morning person. I am not.

What I fail to comprehend is our bizarre interaction first thing every weekend morning (and Statutory holidays, and all the other days when he's not off to work at a ridiculous hour.)

"Good morning," he says, looking up from his computer with a steaming cup of freshly brewed coffee beside him.

"Morning," I mutter (muttering is the best I can do until there's caffeine racing through my body.)

As I pour the dark liquid into the mug that Ger has thoughtfully placed in front of the coffeemaker, I hear him hollering from the living room. (He says he never hollers, but in the morning, if you're not muttering, you're hollering.)

"The dogs have both peed, Max has…" he hollers again. I don't hear the rest of it because I'm still stirring my coffee and the spoon seems a lot louder than it needs to be. To be honest, I don't care what he's hollering about. The house doesn't seem to be on fire.

With coffee in hand, I head into the living room. "What?" I ask as pleasantly as I can. (I am aware I can sound a bit snappy before my coffee, so I try and at least take the edge off. I'm not entirely horrible.)

"Both dogs have peed. Max has pooped, but Jake hasn't, I think he's waiting for you." He says again. Only this time he sounds like he's talking to a three-year-old child with a hearing problem.

"Probably," I mutter.

Why does he insist on giving me a full report on our dogs' urine and fecal output first thing in the morning? I have never shown an interest in it (at least I don't think I have.)

Explaining this habit to my sister, I fully expected her to commiserate with me despite her being a morning person.

"I do that too," she said.

Wait. What?

"What do you mean 'you do that too'?"

"The first thing I tell J every morning is whether the dog has peed or pooped."

"Why?" I asked, expecting an answer that perhaps made perfect sense and I just hadn't thought about it before.

"I have no idea," she replied.

"Seriously?"

"I'm serious. I have no idea why I do that, but for some reason, I thought he would want to know."

People are weird.

Taming Crazy

10. It's All About You Until It Isn't!

What do you mean, it's not all about me?

Self-awareness had already taught me so much, but discovering the ego had the most significant and profound effect on me. I'd always thought the ego was about pride and vanity—and although I confess to having a little of both—I didn't think it was responsible for how I thought about most things in life.

I associated ego with people like Donald Trump and the prolific *selfie-takers* whose self-worth seemed to depend on the number of likes, loves, or comments they received. Validation always seemed to have a price, and I'll confess there were times when I checked my phone more often than I'd like to admit, just to see if someone loved me enough to like something I posted on social media.

I didn't think I was a particularly selfish person. I believed in kindness and compassion most of the time—unless someone pissed me off—then I was fierce.

(Although it was more likely I'd shut down entirely and slink off to a dark corner and lick my emotional wounds.)

It was difficult to believe it was my ego that determined how I thought about everything and could well be the source of my suffering.

Several years ago, I heard about the book *A New Earth* by Eckhart Tolle. Oprah Winfrey had made it one of her book club recommendations and although his book didn't sound like my kind of thing—if Oprah liked it—it was worth giving it a shot.

Usually, anything with a 'new age' label, had me running in the opposite direction, but we were going on a beach holiday soon, and I needed a new book to take along. I found *A New Earth* difficult to read at the time. I understood most of what Mr. Tolle was saying, but it didn't connect with me, and I left the book at the hotel. (I believe laying on that Cuban beach under a palapa drinking fruity cocktails all afternoon probably wasn't the best time to read this kind of material.)

A few years had passed since then, and I was now ready and open to new ideas, so I purchased the book again. Perhaps my mindset had already changed for the better because when I started reading it for the second time, it made sense to me. Here was a man who had suffered from anxiety, depression and thoughts of suicide yet he had made his own way through.

He had saved himself.

This was what I was looking for.

One of the valuable lessons you learn in mindfulness meditation is how to separate yourself from your thoughts. A concept that seemed utterly beyond my capabilities just a few short months before. I had learned not to attach to thought. To let it float through and merely observe it. This means that if we are capable of watching the thought, then it also means that we are not our thoughts. We are only the observer of thought. (This may sound completely *woo-woo* right now but stay with me, I've got you.)

When I first read this theory in Tolle's *A New Earth* while laying on that sandy beach years ago, it was a bit too 'far out there' for me to believe. Now, having experienced the concept first hand, I was convinced of two things:

One:

I am merely the observer of my thoughts.

(Which raises the question; If I'm the observer of my thoughts, who the hell is creating them?)

Two:

The ego creates thoughts.

(Not all of them, but the ego is responsible for most of the bullshit thoughts that cause emotional pain and suffering.)

Take a moment to fully absorb that. I'll wait.

To understand this concept, I needed to look at the ego as a separate entity and saw that it was responsible for all my emotional suffering. The problem was I needed to find a simple way of knowing when my ego was steering the ship into stormy waters, or driving the train off the rails, or leading the march into dangerous territory…

I discovered that the easiest way for me to spot the ego-driven thought was by noticing when my thoughts contained 'I,' 'Me,' or 'My.'

Every time I was thinking; *What about me? I can't do that. You hurt my feelings. Poor me. Blah, blah, blah…* I was thinking with my ego. I had allowed my ego to take control of my thoughts without being aware of it.

What do you mean it's not all about me?

The more I researched this concept, the more fascinated I became, and I learned that this *ego-centric* thinking is normal human behaviour. Humans tend to be egotistical creatures by nature. But why do some of us have egos that hurt and cause emotional pain and suffering? After all, I believed my ego was miles away from someone like Donald Trump—and although it was nowhere near Mother Teresa's—I thought it was at least somewhere in the normal range.

Why was mine causing such anguish, and could changing how I interacted with my ego make a difference?

"Ger," I yelled from the kitchen when I heard the front door opening. I should have waited until he had taken off his coat and hung it in the hallway closet. I should have waited until he had taken off his shoes and placed them in their usual spot on the shelf. I should have at least waited until he had entered the kitchen where I would smile and say, 'Hi honey, how was your day?' I should have waited for him to answer and then share my news.

That's what I should have done.

"Why are you yelling like that?" he asked as he entered the kitchen. Now, to be fair, I'd been sitting at the kitchen table all day and had only gotten up off my ass once every so often to make a cup of tea. I hadn't eaten and the whole day seemed to have gotten away from me, but none of that mattered because I had just had a breakthrough and was splitting at the seams with excitement.

"Sorry, didn't mean to yell," I replied. Normally, I wasn't a yeller. It was just that my head was full of bright flashes from all the lightbulb moments I'd had that day. It was swimming in brilliance, and I needed to share it with him before I drowned in it. (Look at the ego on her. It's as big as a bus.)

As I turned to face him, ready to share my news, he disappeared up the stairs towards the bedroom. *Sigh.*

Waiting patiently, I could feel my enthusiasm slowly dwindling with every passing minute.

"What's up with you?" he said, bending down to kiss my forehead before turning his attention to the fridge.

He knew just by looking around the kitchen that supper wasn't a priority for me today and it would be hastily thrown together at the last minute. Thankfully, he was used to it, and it didn't seem to bother him too much (or at least not enough to attempt to make it himself anyway.)

"You need to sit down. I need your undivided attention," I said, as the dogs continued to jump around and paw at his legs until he couldn't ignore them any longer. He got up again and headed to the cupboard to get the dogs a treat. This was getting painful now.

"Okay," he said sitting back down. "I'm listening. Honestly, I am." He added when he saw the look on my face.

"Okay, good. Tell me if this makes sense."

I shared with him what I thought seemed like a simplified way to look at the ego and why it mattered. I explained how we're all born with an ego and that it's like a protective shell that envelopes us and attempts to keep us safe. It's that little voice in our head that says, *don't go in there, it's not safe.* The voice we ignore when it says, *it's probably not a good idea to try rollerblades for the first time while you're standing on an incline.* (This may or may not have happened.)

The ego is like our voice of reason and common sense. It can boost us up and give us confidence. It's the voice in our head that says, *I can do this,* or *I am going to finish writing this book,* or any other encouragement you may need. These types of thoughts are ego-based, but they keep us moving forward. They're helpful, and we benefit from them.

High five that ego!

The problem is we have never been taught that the ego isn't who we are, so we listen to it and allow it to control us. The ego makes you feel like every situation is all about you and the more you listen to it—the stronger your ego gets. Over time—instead of protecting you and boosting your self-confidence—it can become your biggest source of suffering.

For some of us, it can become very harmful and cause great emotional pain. The voice in your head that started out trying to keep you safe now has two friends—*fear and self-doubt*—and together they're a bloody nightmare.

Fear and self-doubt use your inner stories to strengthen their voices and the more you listen to them—the stronger and louder they become. The ego—joined by fear and self-doubt—can eat away any self-confidence you may have.

I can't do it, so why bother trying.

I'm going to fail.

People will judge me.

How will this affect me?
What will people say about me?
No one ever listens to me.

You may think these thoughts prevent you from getting hurt, but it's the opposite. These voices keep you stuck. They keep you small and the more you listen to them, the more harmful they get. They become your default thinking.

These thoughts hurt you the most because if thoughts create emotions—how can you possibly feel good about yourself if you always think you're not good enough?

Why bother trying if you are going to fail anyway?

"If we think these kinds of thoughts all the time, how can we expect to feel positive or happy? Does that make sense?" I asked, hoping Ger was still following me.

"Yes, but we don't all think the same way so how can you tell the difference between a regular thought and an ego-driven one?" he asked.

"I think the simplest way to tell is whether it contains *I, Me,* or *My.*"

"What do you mean?"

"Anytime you insert yourself into the thought, you're thinking with your ego mind, and I think the easiest way to know you're doing that is by looking at the thought and seeing if you're using *I, Me,* or *My*—or some variation of that."

"Okay, but you said not all 'I, Me, or My' thoughts are harmful, so how does knowing this help you?"

Ger had never suffered from anxiety. I needed to make sure my explanation made sense to him. He was a logical thinker.

If I could explain it in a way he would understand, then there would be a good chance it would be clear for everyone else too. Most of us battling worry and anxiety are over thinkers. We think. We rethink. Then we think about everything all over again. Knowing when a thought is damaging or causing us to suffer, can make all the difference. If we had a simple way to know when our ego had taken over, we would have the opportunity to change it—before it hurt us.

We could stop the suffering.

When I was in the middle of worrying about something my mind went into overdrive. I needed a quick and easy process to get myself out of it. The faster, the better—not only for my benefit—but for everyone else around me.

If someone had said to me 'Stop inserting yourself into your thoughts,' I would be wondering what the hell they were talking about. But the truth is—anytime I worry—I'm making it all about me. Even though that isn't my intention.

Just a quick *I, Me, My* check can stop me from continuing down that road. I don't have to discuss it or justify it—the evidence is right there. The more attention I paid to my negative thoughts, the more I recognized that my ego was usually in control. This was a tough pill to swallow at first. It was obviously going to take some practice.

As I began to accept this concept of the ego, it became easier to identify when I was thinking with it. There were times when my ego helped me move forward—those were the times when I felt pretty good about something I had done.

Then there were times when my ego took over negatively, and I felt myself falling down the rabbit hole of worry, self-doubt, and fear.

I couldn't help but wonder how many decisions I had made in my life that were driven by my ego but quickly decided it was best to let sleeping dogs lie. I wasn't ready to venture into that—at least not yet.

I could envision the ego like a filter on a photograph. When I was thinking in the present—without judging or attaching—the picture was clear, bright, and harmless. But when I applied the ego filter, it changed the picture entirely.

The filters—judgment, shame, doubt, and fear—distorted the picture and the more filters I applied, the more it looked nothing like the original.

After several days of identifying the ego in my own thought process, I grew tired of myself (yes, weird, I know.) I needed to test this theory on someone else—Sista!

Sista would be my test subject. It was a small price to pay for showing up at a time when my four-year-old self thought she was living the good life as an only child. It's the price she pays for being a pain in my ass all those years and putting a severe dent in my childhood social life.

She says she's more than made up for it.

She thinks we're even.

She's probably right.

I had already shared the latest ego discovery with her, so she knew what it was, but I hadn't tested it on her. I wanted to see if it could be applied to anyone. It was time for a field test, and the perfect opportunity popped up one morning while on our way to a meeting.

"Morning, how are you?" I asked as she slid into the passenger seat and buckled herself in.

"I'm good. How are you?" she answered.

This was a typical conversation. The sort of thing people said to each other all the time, but for us, it was how we tested each other's mood. My dislike for small-talk was something I tried to work on. (Just like my lower back when I sat at the computer all day, if I didn't work the kinks out it would get tight and painful. The same thing applied to small talk.)

There was something in the way she answered this morning that didn't seem quite right. She was a morning person, the type that gets up at five every morning to go to the gym (ugh, I know, right?) Her answer to my question wasn't unusual, but her tone sure was. I wasn't used to her morning energy level being as low as mine.

"What's the matter?" I asked. She was wearing dark sunglasses and staring down the long endless highway that stretched out in front of us.

"I'm just tired. Buster isn't doing well," she answered. "Remember I told you we were taking him to the vet?"

"Yeah, of course."

"Well, he told us there's nothing we can do for him, and it was time to let him go. He seemed fine for the last few days but then last night he couldn't get up. I had to carry him outside to go pee. He's not eating or drinking, but the thing is he'll probably be fine tomorrow. I don't know what to do."

"Oh, I'm sorry, that's hard."

She reached down and took out a crumpled tissue from her bag and blotted the tears that were escaping from beneath her oversized sunglasses and running down her cheeks.

"What if he recovers? He seems happy most of the time, he still wags his tail when I talk to him. In some ways, he's the same old Buster, but I know he's in pain," she said.

"What did the vet say you should do?"

"He said it was up to us, but I can't make that decision. He's a big part of the family. I can't imagine him not being there every day. He's my baby."

For the next few minutes, we both stared at the road ahead, neither of us knowing what to say.

"What if this isn't about you?" I blurted out before I could stop myself.

Shit. That didn't sound very comforting or helpful.

"What do you mean?" she said, turning to face me. I kept my eyes firmly focused on the road ahead.

How do I explain this without making everything worse?

"What if this decision isn't about you at all? What if this is about Buster, but you're making it about you?"

She turned away to face the passenger window.

Fuck. The last thing I wanted to do was hurt her. I wanted this information to help her, but now I was starting to have some serious doubts.

"You're right," she said, as she turned to look at me.

I quickly glanced at her and could see that her face had softened. I smiled at her because I knew she got it.

"I was thinking with my ego, wasn't I?" she said as she took off her glasses.

"Yes, but nobody wants to make a decision like that. It would be easier if the vet made it. What the hell do we pay them for anyway?" I said, hoping to lighten the conversation.

"Yes, it would," she said. "I know what you meant though when you said this wasn't about me. I guess I couldn't see it."

"We're never ready to let go, and we definitely don't want to be the one to make a decision like that. It's too painful."

I was relieved that she got it. Not just for her sake but for mine too. I'd been talking about how the ego works for the last few weeks and when I discovered something—I couldn't shut up about it. I shared everything with her, and this time it had paid off.

She knew this wasn't about her.

This was about what was right for Buster, and it somehow made calling the vet a little easier. Two days later she called and told me that he was gone.

"Are you okay?" I asked, knowing how difficult this had been for her.

"I'm good. I'm not going to lie, it was really hard, but I'm okay. It was the right decision for Buster, and that makes it easier to live with, you know?"

"I do."

"Thanks, Sista," she said.

"For what?"

"For sharing all this with me. If you hadn't fallen apart and put yourself back together, I might have still been agonizing over the decision."

"You're welcome... I think."

Over the next few months, Sista and I became self-professed experts at knowing when our own egos showed up. We could also spot the ego in other people from a mile away.

Ger learned to recognize it too. When we walked the dogs after work, we talked about our day and situations where we thought ego played a part. He said that knowing this information made him pause before reacting. It helped him see when people were thinking with their ego mind and why they were making decisions based on how it affected them—instead of what was best for the team or business.

My sister and I noticed the same things too.

It was like the three of us were playing a game called *Spot the Ego* and only we knew we were playing it.

Taming Crazy

11. A Win Is A Win

I emptied my suitcase of all assumptions, and it was considerably lighter to carry. For once in my life, I let logic lead the way.

We were in the middle of another season of severe wild-fires in our province. Our Summers were usually hot and dry, and wildfires were something to be expected. So, when I received a text from our youngest son that included a picture of a looming cloud of dense black smoke approaching his work site, I knew immediately it was a wildfire.

'Where are you?' I texted back.

He was often travelling for work, and I'd grown accustomed to not always knowing where he was. (I had learned to keep a small, comfortable distance from my adult sons. I never wanted my worry to suffocate them or affect them in any way.)

As soon as he replied with his location, I knew immediately this was a problem. How big of a problem, I didn't know—but for me—this was a problem.

That morning, I had watched the wildfires update on the news. There were several large fires in a remote area, and they were out of control. This wasn't something I was concerned about because of their remote location. However, this was too close for comfort because there was a gas plant right in the path of what turned out to be three raging wildfires and my son was right in the middle of it.

The company had already started evacuating people from the plant, but due to the large number of employees involved, the evacuations would take some time. Standard procedure I told myself. No need to worry just yet. But as usual, my mind had its own agenda.

How did I not know he was there?

Why did my son have to be there of all places?

What if something terrible happens to him?

I felt the small gnawing sensation in the pit of my stomach, and it grew with every passing minute. My heart thumped wildly in my chest, and I knew my body was doing what it always did in times like these—it was becoming anxious.

I texted my son again. 'Are you out yet? When are you getting out?' And waited for what seemed like an eternity for him to reply.

'No, I'm not. I don't know when.'

Every time I attempted to write a new text to him, I deleted it and paced around the room instead. I didn't want him to know I was worried (even though he knew I would be.)

It was what I always did. I worried.

I kept the television on in the background hoping for an update, but they kept showing the same thing over and over.

"Tell me something I don't already know," I shouted at the telly, and within seconds a wildfire update website address scrolled across the bottom of the screen. Grabbing my laptop,

I quickly typed the address into the search bar and scrolled through page after page trying to find new information. I'm not sure what I expected to see exactly but every word I read only fueled my anxiety. I was standing on the edge, peering down into the anxiety rabbit hole—preparing for the darkness—when something made me reach out and stop the fall.

I paused.

That pause gave me time to breathe.

I was used to barely breathing at times like these. Shallow, empty breaths that seemed to accompany worry and fear. This time, I paused and breathed as deeply as I could and felt a sense of calmness wash over me.

This situation wasn't about me.

My ego had pushed me in the wrong direction. I had taken the worry route. Worry wasn't going to help anyone right now. I needed to do something constructive and find my way back to the fork in the road—back to the beginning. I picked up my phone and texted my son again.

'Sweetheart, please stay safe and keep me updated.'

'I will mum,' he replied.

I knew if I continued to wait for information, I would be battling my ego all day, but I couldn't focus on work either. I needed to do something to help quiet the voices that kept popping into my head. I picked up the phone and called Ger. He would know what to say and what to do in this situation.

Ger explained that everyone who worked in the plant was well trained, including our son who was smart, rational, and good at his job. He described the safety plans in detail and how these plants had to accommodate for this type of thing. They would have an emergency plan in place. Even in worst case scenarios (which of course was where my mind was going), he would be okay because they had everything there for his survival. He would be safe. He would be fine.

Ger answered every question I had, and even though I knew some of them were irrational—instead of continuing to assume the worse like I normally did—I believed him!

Listening to him explain all the procedures had helped to calm the inner voices. I found myself in a place I wasn't used to—in control of my thoughts. I was still concerned about our son, but the worry, the panic, and the anxiety had started to melt away. My ego had told me this was all about me, but it wasn't—it never was.

In the past, I would have spent the entire day fixated on the wildfire update site. But now—knowing all the facts about the situation—I was able to bury myself in my work. I focused on my to-do list. I got things done.

A few hours later, my son sent a message that he was still inside the plant, but he was safe and hoped to be evacuated the next day.

'Don't worry mum. I'm safe.'

When you're a worrier, just uttering the words 'don't worry' is like saying 'don't eat all the chocolate in front of you.' I'm going to do it.

'Don't worry,' is a green light to worry.

The worry train always stops at my station, and while I'm standing on the platform, all I hear is 'All aboard.'

I took my usual seat in the front of the worry train, and I never missed a trip. I had a bird's eye view and absorbed every concern, assumption, fear, and pain I saw along the way. The train always reached its destination—it crashed and burned—ultimately taking me along with it.

This time, I had climbed aboard the train—but instead of taking my usual seat—I had turned around and jumped off at the first opportunity. My suitcase was filled with knowledge instead of assumption, and it was considerably lighter to carry. For once in my life, I let logic lead the way.

Later that day, I made a cup of tea and sat down with a notebook and pen. I wrote down some of the thoughts I had earlier in the day.

Why hasn't my son been evacuated yet?
Why does my son have to be there of all places?
Not knowing is killing me.

I never realized worrying about my son said more about me than him. My thoughts were ego driven, but when I removed the ego and looked at the situation logically and rationally (something I never thought possible), it changed how I felt. It didn't mean I didn't love my son with all my heart. It didn't mean I wasn't concerned about him. It just meant I was no longer willing to let my ego control me or the situation.

I was more effective if I was fully present, not drowning in the *But What If* cesspool I usually fell in to. This must be how people like Ger felt.

It felt like peace.

Early the next morning, I received a text from my son.

'Probably be evacuated today.'

I wasn't happy he was still there, but I knew he would be okay. I buried myself in my work and trusted he would let me know if anything changed. Later that evening he messaged that he was home.

This incident doesn't seem all that significant on the surface, but for me it was huge. It was an indication that I had turned a corner. All the hard work of paying attention to my thoughts and emotions was paying off. If I hadn't changed how I thought about the situation—if I had continued down the route I'd always travelled—this whole ordeal would have sidelined me. Worry would have continued to build, and anxiety would have taken control. I would have spent those two days in complete emotional agony.

A win is a win, no matter how small it may seem!

12. I Can See Clearly Now

You can see the world more clearly when your windows are clean.

The lessons I had already learned made a big impact on how I saw everything—including myself—but it was time to move on. To take it further.

Patience had never been a strength of mine unless you needed to queue up for something. I'm quite good at queuing. Being British, we learn how to walk, and then we learn how to queue (I think it's a law or something.)

I knew how I felt was dependant on what I was thinking, and my emotion determined how I behaved, but I needed a way of turning this concept into something simple and tangible that I could use every day.

I needed to create an easy way to remind myself that thoughts created emotions, and emotions drove our actions. That's when I realized it was right in front of me the whole time… **T.E.A.**

What on earth could be easier than TEA?

I say nothing. The answer is nothing!

T Thought.

What you think about a situation, event, or person.

E Emotion.

How you feel when you think about something.

A Action.

How you react or behave when you feel a certain way. Sometimes it's inaction but is still driven by how you feel. (Like not getting your ass off the sofa when you're unhappy or overwhelmed.)

And there it was. Not exactly ground-breaking or anything that hasn't been said before, but one acronym was all it took to clear away the cobwebs. It made sense to me, and I was excited to see how it would work in the real world. In my world.

"Good morning," the Boss said, as he stood in the doorway of my office.

"Morning," I replied, barely looking up from my computer. I had four email inboxes to sort through, a growing stack of 'priorities' on my desk, urgent messages to respond too, and a sick staff member. I didn't have time for small talk—which I didn't particularly enjoy at the best of times—I certainly had no time for it today.

"Are you busy?" he asked.

What the hell. Can't you see I'm up to my eyeballs here?

"Sort of. Do you need something?"

"Yes. Sorry, I asked Sheila to do it, but I guess she didn't have time and I need it today," he said, handing me an over-stuffed file folder.

This was standard procedure. His way of solving a problem was to make it my problem. My workload was piling up, and I was already feeling frustrated, overwhelmed, and just plain fed up. It was barely eight-thirty on a Monday morning.

This was more common than I cared to admit. The situation could be slightly different, but the result would always be the same. I was frustrated, overwhelmed, and pissed off. It was a feeling I had much too frequently—and even though I no longer worked in the office fulltime—I still often felt this way.

It was something I wanted to change.

Like most people, I spent a significant part of my day at my job. Perhaps this was the perfect opportunity to put the T.E.A. theory into practice. After all, how I felt about my job wasn't going to change unless I did something about it.

Feeling slightly lifted by the possibility that I could change how I thought and felt, I grabbed a fresh cup of coffee and headed to my desk. Closing my laptop and putting my phone on silent—I felt lighter almost immediately.

This must be how it feels to have a plan.

I wrote T E A down the left-hand side of a sheet of paper. Next to the E, I wrote FRUSTRATED. This was an emotion I was familiar with. I knew how it felt in my body. Every muscle in my body tightened. My shoulders crept up towards my ears. My neck and back ached, and my stomach tensed. By the time I finished work, my head would be pounding.

These signs had been building for years, but I was paying attention now. I could clearly see it.

Looking at the A, I thought about what I did when I was feeling frustrated at work. Complain to my co-worker, bitch to my sister, and vent to my husband came to mind. Sometimes—when the frustration had reached its boiling point—I could be irritable. I would bite my tongue when I thought someone wasn't doing something I thought they should. When someone asked what I thought was a stupid question, I told myself I had a low threshold for stupidity (which makes me sound terribly obnoxious, but I'm truth-telling, and the truth isn't always pretty!) I wrote VENT next to the A.

I kept the T for last because I knew this was going to be uncomfortable. Shining a light on what you're thinking can be difficult. If people could hear what I was really thinking, I'm sure I would have been locked up long ago or at least heavily sedated. I took a deep breath and started writing. The truth.

T Why do I always have to do EVERYTHING?
I must have SUCKER written on my forehead.
This place would fall apart without ME.
I really HATE this job.

E FRUSTRATED

A VENT!!!!!

Staring at the words in front of me, I wondered how many times I thought and felt that way in the past week, month, year. I didn't know, but it was becoming much too frequent. I often thought of packing it all in, finding a new job that I would happily get out of bed in the morning for. (Who am I kidding? Not much will get me out of bed happily.)

Instead of doing something about it, I had complained, bitched, and vented. Sometimes, I didn't share it with anyone, but inside I'd be seething.

There were times when as soon as Ger walked in the door after work, I poured out all my frustrations and instantly felt better when he agreed with me. Validation always feels good. When he didn't agree with me, I would think it was because he didn't understand.

He had no clue what I had to put up with.

Of course, everything would get better for a while—until something set it off again—and the cycle would continue. I noticed it was getting more frequent as I got older and thought it was because my patience was wearing thin.

Looking back on my reaction to frustration, I saw that I blamed my job, my employer, my co-workers, the weather, the doorman (I don't have a doorman, but I imagine I would blame him if I had one).

One thing was glaringly obvious—I never blamed myself! No. Two things were glaringly obvious—I never blamed myself, and this wasn't about blame.

It was about ego!

So, there it was. The truth in front of me in black and white.

I took a deep breath and looked at what I had written...

Why do I always have to do EVERYTHING?
Hello, ego. You make me believe that I do everything, but that's not true, is it?

I must have SUCKER written on my forehead.
I didn't have SUCKER written on my forehead. (I would have noticed when I looked in the mirror this morning especially now that my bangs have grown out.)

This place would fall apart without ME.
Some other obnoxious person must have written this. It doesn't sound like me at all.

I HATE this job.
Ugh. I hate the word hate. How bloody melodramatic can you get? I don't hate my job. I like quite a lot of it in fact. I even liked the people there most of the time. There were just parts of it I disliked sometimes, and there were times when I had allowed that dislike to become overwhelming.

I sat there for a moment and realized that I was smiling which was quite surprising since my mouth doesn't usually do that when I'm frustrated. (Perhaps it was a grimace, but let's just say I was smiling—it sounds far nicer.) Just by questioning every thought I had written down, I already felt better. The situation was still the same, but I no longer felt weighed down with frustration. The only thing that had changed was my thoughts about it.

It was clear I was taking my job too personally. It was a job, and it was a good one. I needed to look at it differently.

When asked to take on extra assignments, perhaps it was because I was capable of it and not because I was a 'sucker.' I needed to start delegating especially if I thought I was doing too much and was feeling overwhelmed or frustrated. I needed to rethink my entire world.

I needed to stop assuming.

I couldn't wait to tell Ger about my new acronym and eagerly waited for him to get home that evening.

"Hi honey," he said as he waltzed in through the front door. (He says he didn't waltz in and that he just walked in but I'm the one telling the story, so I win.)

"Hi," I replied, a little too high pitched than I would have liked. I followed him into the kitchen and watched as he gave the dogs their treats (for no reason other than just being dogs.)

"I have so much to tell you," I squealed (yes, I'm sure it was a squeal.) Obviously, I needed to share my news before I lost my composure completely.

"Ok. I'll just go up and change clothes first," he said and headed up the stairs to the bedroom.

Sigh.

I waited. Again.

The moment he stepped back into the kitchen I hit him with all my news. How I felt. What I thought. How I used T.E.A. to turn everything around. When I finished, he was smiling.

"That's great," he said. "All your hard work is paying off."

"I know, right. Who knew I had such a big ego?"

"Well…" he started to say before I shut him down.

Practicing self-awareness meant I no longer allowed negative thoughts—especially the ego-centric ones—to control how I felt. If I noticed a thought creating unnecessary negativity—I questioned it, and it would usually dissipate quickly. Not every single time (I'm far from perfect) but it did become easier. I even started to enjoy my work again. (I still didn't get up in the morning with a smile on my face or a bounce in my step, but you can't have everything!)

Ger and I had started meeting downtown for lunch once a week. (Apparently, I needed a weekly reminder that I could be out in public and function quite well.) I looked forward to these weekly outings, but I discovered that my heightened self-awareness also had it's down-side. It created a fascination in watching the behaviour of other people.

"I wonder what he's feeling right now?" I asked Ger as we walked down the street behind a man who was screaming into his phone.

"Who knows. I'm starving. Where do you want to eat?"

Ger didn't always share my enthusiasm for human nature. I would point out behaviours, but my excitement in watching other people didn't always translate into his excitement for some reason. Some things are best kept to myself I thought (making a mental note to tell my sister about it later.)

"You bloody idiot," I screamed, as the little blue car cut sharply in front of me forcing me to slam on my brakes to avoid hitting him. Thankfully, the vehicle behind me had managed to do the same. The little blue car sped away, darting in and out of traffic as it went.

I was furious.

I was having a perfectly reasonable day until that stupid bloody idiot came along. *He doesn't give a shit about anyone but himself*, I thought as I felt anger start to build up inside me. The more I thought about what could have happened, the tighter I gripped the steering wheel. By the time I arrived at my appointment my whole body was tense, my stomach was churning, my arms were sore, and my shoulders and neck were aching. I didn't feel very good at all.

"What's the matter with you?" Ger asked when I arrived home later that day.

"Nothing," I replied as I threw my bag on the kitchen table.

"You look upset."

"I'm fine. I'm just tired."

"Right," he said, nodding his head.

He knew I wasn't fine or tired. It was my usual answer when I didn't feel like explaining myself. It was a legitimate response even if it was a lazy one.

As I cooked supper, it occurred to me that I still wasn't in the best of moods. That little blue car had cut me off at least two hours earlier, but I was still feeling a little 'pissed off.' I wasn't angry—anger had dissipated hours ago—but I was still feeling... something.

Was I still blaming that little blue car—or more specifically, the asshole driver of the little blue car—for how I was feeling right now? Damn!

Taking out my notepad and pen, I sat at the kitchen table. At the top of the page, I wrote down the situation—which was quite simply—ASSHOLE CUT ME OFF!

I wrote T E A down the side of the page and emptied my brain onto the paper. By the time I was done, I had over-cooked the spaghetti.

"Supper's ready!"

"What's all this?" Ger asked as he walked into the kitchen.

At first, I thought he meant the sad, limp noodles on his plate. But soon realized he meant the notes I'd hastily shoved to the side when I noticed the pasta sauce was burning.

"I'm processing what happened today."

"Why? What happened today?"

"Some asshole cut me off, and I'm trying to process why it affected me."

"That's good," he said, as he vigorously salted his pasta.

"What do you mean 'That's good'?"

"I mean it's good that you're working on it. People cut me off in traffic all the time. They're idiots. I just don't let it spoil my whole day."

We can't all be perfect like you my darling, I thought as I shoved a forkful of spaghetti into my mouth. We ate in silence. I was too busy thinking to talk, and I imagine Ger was thankful for the reprieve and enjoyed the peace.

After supper, Ger retreated to the living-room, while I sat back at the kitchen table and looked at my notes.

ASSHOLE CUT ME OFF!

T   The idiot almost hit me.
    He doesn't give a shit about anyone else.
    He's an asshole.

I was lucky I saw him.
How the fuck does he have a licence?
If I hadn't stopped in time....

E Pissed off. Mad. Angry.

A Gripped the steering wheel too tightly.
(My neck hurts, and I have a headache.)

RESULT: Body hurts!!! Bad mood!!!!

I could have written a lot more, but I didn't need to. Seeing the process written down it was all glaringly obvious. I had turned an ordinary everyday traffic incident into something that not only fueled my mood, but it had affected my whole body.

I could see it so clearly now.

Taming Crazy

13. We're All Fine

We're always fine until we're not.

"Morning Jess," I said, as she strode past me in the hallway almost knocking the bundle of files out of my hands.

"Sorry," she said as she rushed to the staffroom still dressed in her winter coat and boots.

Jess was never late for work. She was one of those people who were first to arrive and last to leave. She was dependable and good at her job. The type of woman that said what she thought. Jess didn't play games or beat around the bush, she walked right up to that bush, pushed it aside and walked straight on through. I liked her.

It was obvious something was off with her this morning as she threw her lunch bag in the fridge and took a coffee mug off the shelf. "Damn it," she whispered, as she picked up the coffee pot and poured the last dregs of coffee into the sink. Pulling out the coffee filter holder, she slammed it against the inside of the garbage bin, dislodging, not only the used soggy filter but the entire holder along with it. As she fished into the garbage to retrieve the holder and vigorously rinse it under the running tap water, I could see the tension on her face. Her eyes were red, and the furrowed line between her eyes looked more pronounced than usual. She finished preparing the coffee-maker, switched it on, and stormed out of the room.

A little later Jess headed back to the staff room. I followed her under the pretense of needing coffee (not actually a pretense because… it's coffee!) The room was empty except for the two of us.

"How are you?" I asked.

"Fine," she answered, a little too quickly.

I finished pouring my coffee. "Okay. Well, you know where I am if you want to talk about anything." I smiled at her and walked back to my office. I had an open-door policy even if that meant my work would suffer or I ended up taking on more problems than I needed too. The truth was, I enjoyed solving problems or at least attempting to.

At lunchtime, I walked into the staffroom and saw Jess sitting alone at the kitchen table eating what looked like soggy leftovers from an orange stained plastic container. She looked up, and as she caught my eye, she smiled.

"I'm sorry about this morning," she said.

"That's alright. We all have those mornings."

I had no idea what Jess was going through. She was usually an open book and one of those people that seemed to have her shit together (but then again, people thought that about me too.)

"Things just got to me this morning. I don't usually let stuff bother me, but sometimes they just pile up, you know what I mean?" she said, blowing her nose in her napkin.

Nodding, I sat down at the table across from her. I wanted to test the TEA theory on someone, and Jess was right there. She was an ideal subject, but she was also an unknowing one. I remembered what Ger had said about other people not appreciating my new-found wisdom.

Don't try to fix her!

"Do you want to talk about it?" I asked, ignoring the little voice in my head that told me to mind my own business.

"There's not much to talk about. I feel a bit stupid now, to be honest. I hit my breaking point last night with the kids and probably blew things out of proportion, but damn sometimes I feel like I'm the only one that does everything. Ever feel like you just want to run away from it all?"

"Only all the time." I laughed. "When the boys were teenagers, I wanted to strangle them more than a few times."

I knew Jess's husband worked out of town a lot. They had three kids, but I had no idea how old the kids were because I usually shut off when the topic of kids come up. I couldn't even remember her husband's name.

"The kids take advantage when Ryan's not home," she said.

Yes, Ryan, that's right, now I remember.

"So, what happened last night?" I asked.

"Things just piled up, I guess. We were so busy here yesterday and then I had to deal with that awful person on the phone just before we left, so that didn't help. Then on the way home, I stopped at the store to pick up a few things it was so busy, and of course, there were only two tills open. By the time I got to the front of the line, I was already ticked off. Then the girl couldn't scan the package of cheese and said she had to call someone. I said, 'Forget it, I don't want the damn cheese.' Which makes me feel like a complete bitch because I know it wasn't her fault." She blew her nose again. "By the time I got home, I was in a bad mood."

I nodded, but before I could respond, she continued.

"I walked into the kitchen, and it was a disaster, I mean it's always messy I admit but this was a complete mess. Nobody had bothered to put their dishes in the dishwasher or even in the sink. The bowls had dried cereal stuck to them. There were spots of peanut butter and jam all over the counter where they'd been making sandwiches after school, and they'd left the bread bag open and left the milk out."

"Oh boy," I said before I could stop myself. I was trying to sound sympathetic, but instead, it sounded pathetic. I'm not even an 'Oh boy' kind of person (maybe I thought that's how a reasonable person would have responded.) Thankfully, she didn't seem to notice.

"Oh, there's more," she said as she reached for a Kleenex. "I'd spent the morning folding laundry, putting it in separate piles on the sofa for the kids to put away. I told them to make sure they had taken their laundry to their rooms and put them away properly before they left for school. Of course, they hadn't done that. When I got home and saw their friends eating our food while sitting on the clean laundry, I'd had enough." Jess wiped away a tear from the corner of her left eye. "Anyway, I lost my temper. I don't remember what I said, all I remember was the look on my kid's faces. I'm ashamed of myself. I didn't even make them supper. I just locked myself in my room. I must have fallen asleep right away because I didn't wake up until my alarm went off this morning. Caleb had already left for school by the time I came downstairs, and the other two left as soon as they saw me. They didn't even say goodbye."

She took another handful of tissues from the box beside her and dabbed at the tears that had now spilled down her cheeks.

"I'm sorry," she said quietly, "I don't usually let things get to me like this. I'm fine now."

"That's good," I replied.

I thought about all the times I had felt like Jess when life piled up and overwhelmed me. I wanted her to feel like she wasn't alone. Spilling your guts at work was hard enough, without feeling like you might be judged for it.

I wanted to make sure I said the right thing especially when she probably had more on her plate than she was letting on. But before I could say anything else, a few more people entered the room, effectively killing the conversation. Jess smiled at me and continued eating her lunch as if nothing had happened. The usual lunchtime chatter filled the air, but I wasn't listening. I was too busy going over Jess's situation in my head. I finished my lunch and headed back to my office.

Jess had given me much to think about. She had dealt with a lot of things yesterday, and I was going to try and break it into separate issues to make sense of it. I took out a fresh sheet of paper from my desk drawer and wrote down each situation she had mentioned during our conversation.

#1 <u>Rude phone call</u>

T I don't need this right now?
Why do I have to listen to this???

E Frustrated? Overwhelmed? Tired?

A-?

Result – Drove to store already feeling frustrated!!!

#2 **At the store**

T Why is there only 2 till open?
This is ridiculous; I need to get home?
How long do they expect me to wait?

E Frustrated? Angry?

A Rude to the cashier? Left without cheese?

Result – Drove home feeling much more frustrated.

#3 **Home**

T These kids are disrespectful?
Why do I have to do everything around here?
Can't they see I've had a hard day?
Why aren't they helping me?
If they cared at all, they would.

E Unloved? Frustrated? Overwhelmed?

A Locked herself away? Over-reacted? Alienated the kids? Confused them by her reaction?

Result – Took out her frustration on the kids more than she usually would?

#4 <u>Today</u>

T I over-reacted last night, now my kids hate me.
I'm a terrible mother.
I shouldn't have lost my temper.
I embarrassed them in front of their friends

E Ashamed? Guilty?

A Quiet at work? Crying at lunch?

Result – Giving the staff the silent treatment affecting the work atmosphere??

Of course, I had no idea how Jess thought or felt about what had happened, and I didn't want to ask her (at least not yet.) All I could do was to try and put myself in her shoes and make somewhat of an educated guess.

Looking at each situation individually I could see how it wasn't one thing that had Jess feeling like she did. It had accumulated throughout the day. It had become something more significant as the day wore on and had resulted in Jess breaking down.

Is this what happens to all of us?

Does this explain how we let everything snowball until some seemingly little thing happens to tip us over the edge and we fall apart?

How many times over the past few years had I cried to Ger about some insignificant thing, leaving him wondering why I was over-reacting? I always bottled my feelings. Pushing them down into that familiar dark place deep inside (along with all the other emotions I didn't want to deal with.) Sooner or later they overflowed and the last thing in—became the first thing out. Which always seemed to be the little stupid thing.

'I'm fine,' I said when he asked what was wrong.

I was always fine. Until I wasn't.

14. Now What?

"It is the mark of an educated mind to be able to entertain a thought without accepting it." ~*Aristotle*

The more I practiced using TEA—the more fascinated I was by how simple the process could be. I was more self-aware than ever before and felt less encumbered. All the emotional baggage I had always carried around with me was noticeably lighter.

It was almost as if I was looking at life through a different lens (not exactly rose-coloured glasses), but I had wiped away the dust, smudges and fingerprints that used to obstruct my view. It was clear that thoughts created emotions, and those emotions drove actions.

Cause and effect—yes, I get it. But, now what?

Thoughts and over-thinking had always been a problem. I had blamed everything and everyone for my anxieties, my moods, my periods of depression. But it was my thoughts that were the problem all along.

What the hell was I to do about those?

I knew how to identify the initial thought that led me down the garden path, resulting in me lying face down at the bottom of the rabbit hole. But could I prevent that thought from showing up in the first place?

Was that even possible?

Ger often talked about finding the 'root cause' when he was investigating a situation at work. This was kind of the same thing. I needed to find the 'root thought' and find out why it had made an appearance.

Thoughts often ran deep, entwining themselves around all sorts of things, and unravelling them was going to be difficult. I took out the notebook (the one I used to write down all my thoughts when I first started my self-awareness) and realized I had already done most of the work. Reading all the thoughts I had previously written down was a little unsettling at first. Most of my initial thoughts sounded pathetic, dramatic, dark, completely illogical and irrational. I sounded completely insane at times, but I needed to own it. I also needed to remind myself of one of the most important lessons I had learned.

Thoughts are not who I am.

It was apparent that most of my negative, damaging thoughts were running through my head with little or no supervision. I had allowed my ego to take control and steer the ship right into the eye of every storm. He stood on the deck and watched me hang on for dear life as the swell of damaging thoughts engulfed me, Dragging me into its murky depths.

My ego could have easily steered the ship towards calmer waters—but no—he preferred the drama of the high seas. He was used to making decisions on where we went because I had relinquished all my power to him. He had never stopped to ask my opinion, and I never realized I had a say in what direction we sailed. If I had known, I would have stood up and said, 'Excuse me, but I'll take over from here.' I'd lock him in the cargo hold. Steer the ship towards calmer waters and drop anchor in a lovely sunny cove, protected from the storm. (Yes, my ego is male for some reason!)

Thoughts started out innocently enough, but soon the 'What ifs' devoured me.

What if?—The war cry of the worrier!

In the rare times I posted a comment or question on social media, I forced myself not to delete it immediately. Ninety-two percent of the time, I deleted it within an hour because anxiety told me no one would care.

What if people think I'm an idiot for asking such a stupid question?
What if people don't even bother to answer?
Maybe I should delete it before someone sees it.
What if I delete it and people notice I deleted it?
What if, what if, WHAT IF…

When you suffer from these kind of thoughts, intellectually you know they do more harm than good. You know they're unnecessary, totally irrational, almost always illogical, and a complete waste of time (or maybe you don't.) The problem is even though we know they're not good for us, we're at an absolute loss on what to do about them.

'Think positively!'
'Don't worry about it!'
'There's nothing to worry about!'
'Stop worrying!'

It's not as simple as thinking happy thoughts, singing kumbaya, and skipping off into the sunset (or just steering the ship into calmer waters.)

Nobody chooses to worry all the time.

Nobody chooses anxiety.

Telling us not to worry can make us want to poke you in the eye (in a loving way of course because we know you just want to help, but please stop doing it.)

So, now what?

I knew how to pause as soon as I felt an unwanted emotion. I knew its vibrations. I knew how to label the emotion. To identify the thought that had created it, but now I wanted to see if I could do more. I needed to take it even further.

Research had shown that questioning the thought often rendered it harmless and I knew that Byron Katie used this method in her work too. I settled on two simple questions to ask every time a thought was causing emotional anguish, and I needed to pull myself back from falling over the edge.

Question #1 - Is It True?

Is the thought true?

The answer is usually… no.

More often than not, this question changes everything. A lot of our thoughts are not based on fact at all but on assumptions. Those of us dealing with worry and anxiety are useless when it comes to facts (we're way too busy imagining all sorts of scary things.)

Facts, we don't have time for facts!

And there lies the problem.

We listen to the voices in our head and absorb what other people tell us. We interpret these thoughts—add our own little twist of drama and flair—and end up with something else entirely. We take the original thought and fatten it up with our assumptions, beliefs, and inner stories. We ruminate on it and when we have thought about it relentlessly (not intentionally of course) we find ourselves falling down the rabbit hole of despair.

Some of us are experts at this because we've been doing it all our damn lives. Trust me when I say—we're really, really good at it.

The more I asked myself 'Is this true?' The more I realized I often listened to my inner voices when I should have been searching for the truth instead. I assumed the voices in my head were truthful, or at least they were telling me something factual. They never did.

So, before the suffering begins, ask yourself... 'Is this true?'

Question #2 – Am I thinking with my ego?

Is the thought based on ego?

Am I making this all about me?

The answer is yes. You probably are making it about you.

This became one of my favourite questions to ask because the ego is the most significant instigator when it comes to prolonging negative emotions.

Whenever I was feeling bad or sorry for myself—I knew the ego was front and centre. All that anguish and pain is often centred around ourselves in one way or another.

Poor me. Nobody loves me. Nobody cares.

Hey Eeyore, I get it, I really do!

As soon as I removed myself from the thought, everything changed. Most situations were not about me at all, but my ego told me they were. The 'what if' thoughts are almost always ego based.

What if I fail?

What about me?

What if I make a complete and utter fool of myself?

What if I write this book and no one reads it—or even worse—what if they hate it and everyone thinks I'm nuts? (Truthfully, this has become a tough one to shake.)

Captain Ego had been in control for so long that it was easy to follow him down the negativity route. He often had me believing it was all about me. When I start feeling bad about myself—fear, doubt, and worry will set in and before I knew it—anxiety had joined the party. I'd be in a complete state of panic, hiding under my duvet in tears wondering what the hell happened.

Well, suck it up Buttercup. It's not about you!

Of course, I can't forget about the other side of the ego which is responsible for positive thinking.

I'm going to succeed.

I think I did a good job.

I'm proud of myself for writing this book.

I'm sure it will help a few people.

But to be honest, I don't know this side of the ego very well. We're acquaintances, but we don't stop and chat very often. Like most worriers and anxiety sufferers—positive thoughts aren't usually part of my inner dialogue.

Thinking positively isn't my default mode.

Asking a chronic worrier, not to worry or to just think positively, will result in them smiling sweetly. But behind the friendly exterior, there's a scared little girl (or boy) that just wants to run and hide. They may also want to punch you in the face, but mostly they just want to run and hide.

Having the capacity to pause for a moment and question a thought is powerful. Knowing that you are not the thought, but merely the observer of the thought and that you can change it before it damages you is empowering.

I may always have a negative default mode, but now I have the knowledge I need to override that default way of thinking. Just knowing that is comforting. When I'm feeling down, frustrated, overwhelmed, or worried—I can go back and question my thoughts—instead of berating myself and continuing to feel like crap. I can question myself.

Is it true?

You can't handle the truth.

Yes, I can.

Oh, well in that case, no. I made it all up.

Well, then fuck off!

Is Ego here?

Yes, I'm here because it's all about me.

No, it isn't, you're just making it look that way.

Really?

Yes really, so fuck off!

(This is inner dialogue obviously. This conversation will not have the same outcome if said out loud in public. Although it would be a hell of a lot funnier.)

Asking these two simple questions works!

After just a few days of questioning myself, I no longer felt weighed down with troublesome thoughts and emotions. I was able to stay present more often and didn't feel consumed with worry and anxiety.

Meditation continued to help me focus on the present. Which not only helped me stay in the moment, but I felt calmer and mentally stronger than I had ever felt before.

The thoughts that used to send me running for cover no longer had any hold over me because I knew how to separate myself from them. I knew they weren't me!

The key was to look at the thought from the outside looking in. I'd been doing it wrong all these years because I was trying to work through the thoughts from within my head, but doubt, fear, and anxiety always won.

Damaging thoughts are like cockroaches. They come out in the darkness when they think they're alone, feeding on any crumbs of insecurity they can find. Shine a light on them, and they scatter pretty quickly.

Whenever I found myself caught up in a thought that was creating a prolonged negative emotion—I paused.

I examined the thought.

Sometimes it was easy to catch, and within minutes—sometimes seconds—after asking myself the questions, I felt better. I didn't feel the need to judge or blame myself for the way I thought. I no longer beat myself up for worrying because as soon as I became aware I was doing it, I knew I had the power to control it.

And that, my friend, is more empowering than anything I can think of!

As soon as I began looking at thoughts as just thoughts, life became easier. Ger and Sista noticed the difference too—and although I was as crazy as ever—I was still me.

Me without anxiety!

I liked the fact that I was imaginative, creative, sensitive, emotional, and eclectic bordering on eccentric. I didn't want to kill that part of myself. I was more than happy to discover that all this work I had been doing, didn't change who I was. It only changed how I saw the world around me.

How I saw myself.

All these years, I had learned to bottle up my creative side for fear of not being good enough or talented enough, but now I could release it.

Because I am enough.

(According to Ger, some days, I'm more than enough!)

Taming Crazy

15. Into the Deep

Like a small seed dancing across the fertile soil,
it landed softly, but I didn't see it.

"Lets go for a walk."
"I can't."
"Yes, you can."
"I can't. It's too hard."
"You're doing hard things now, remember?"
"You don't understand."
"I know I don't, but I understand you, and you need to go for a walk, so let's go."

In that moment.

I hated him for making me go.

I needed him to make me go.

I loved him for making me go.

Falling into the deep darkness, I was confused.

I had told myself that by learning how to manage my anxiety, I would be fine. I had believed I had this all figured out and it was true. I had conquered anxiety. But depression without anxiety is a different animal altogether.

Years ago, I had visited our family doctor. A small pinched man who never quite seemed to be able to look you in the eye. He preferred to stare squarely at your chest.

"I think I'm depressed," I said.

"Are you suicidal?" He asked.

"No."

"Do you think about hurting yourself?"

"No."

"You're probably just run down. You should try and take it easy for a while. You'll be fine. Come and see me again if it doesn't improve."

"Okay," I replied.

That's all I wanted to hear. It wasn't depression. I was just run down. Mentally and physically, I felt like roadkill, so the diagnosis seemed legitimate.

Yes. I was just rundown. What a relief!

We had two young boys at the time, and Ger often worked out of town. I had no time to acknowledge what was wrong with me. I was just relieved it wasn't depression.

Every time I felt the darkness approaching, I pushed it as far away as I could. There was no time to think of myself when I had two little boys to worry about. But as soon as they were all tucked in for the night, I'd retreat to our bedroom, and everything came flooding out. The next morning I'd put on my brave face and start the day all over again.

My boys were my beautiful distractions.

My boys saved me from me.

Depression without anxiety was unfamiliar, and it scared the hell out of me. The darkness. The oppressive heaviness and endless tears were all there, but this was different.

This was a deep hollow void.

There was nothing to hold on to. No thoughts to attach to. I was floating.

I desperately tried to find a thought I could embrace. I reached out for something, anything. But it was like holding a delicate bubble in the palm of your hand. It disappeared.

I needed a thought to process, but there was nothing.

No worry. No doubt. No fear. Nothing. I was numb.

Like a small seed dancing across the fertile soil, it landed softly, but I didn't see it. As it took root, I ignored it, and it started to sprout. I turned my back on it foolishly believing that acknowledging it would somehow make it true. It grew.

I cried, and I slept.

I told myself I'd be okay in a minute.

In an hour. In a day. Soon.

Days passed and morphed into weeks.

Nothing.

For the first time in my life, I thought about nothing, and it terrified me. I knew I could process thoughts, but I couldn't find one. I was used to racing thoughts—a mind out of control—but this was different.

Something was wrong, and I couldn't shift it.

Ger's concern was palatable. He watched over me.

He kept me safe.

I wanted him to leave me alone, but I needed him to stay.

And he did.

I wanted to drift, but I needed him to be my anchor.

And he was. He always was.

When I drifted too far out and lost sight of the shore, he pulled me back to safety.

He never lost sight of me.

When I shut myself away, hiding under blankets like a wounded animal, he brought me tea and tucked me in.

"Is there something I can do? Is there something you need?" He would ask. Concern etched in his furrowed brow.

"No. I'm okay." I would answer.

He never realized that he was already doing all that he needed to do. He was there. With me.

Until the cloud had lifted.

Until I could shrug off the heaviness.

Until we were back to our usual lives.

Until we were laughing at silly, stupid things again.

Until then, he saves me.

He saves me.

Every time.

16. What's Your Story, Morning Glory?

Our stories begin in childhood, sprinkled with imagination and layered with years of experience, they form the bricks and mortar of who we are.

I have always loved stories. I spent hours reading about the real and fictional lives of other people not realizing that while I was reading someone else's story—I was unknowingly writing my own.

My story wasn't as exciting or adventurous as I had always dreamed it would be. But I had a story nevertheless.

We all do.

There are those special stories we only share with our loved ones and close friends. Less personal stories are reserved for our casual friends and acquaintances. But the important stories—the stories that truly matter—are the ones we tell ourselves when we're alone.

Our stories can seem so real—so true to us—it seems impossible to separate from them no matter how wrong or ridiculous they may seem to others. These stories begin in childhood. Sprinkled with imagination and layered with years of experience, they form the bricks and mortar of who we are.

Our story originates with words we believe to be true and can affect our entire lives. Some may call it a *belief system* but try and start a conversation with 'What's your belief system?' and you may be written off as a weirdo—someone to be avoided at all costs.

These beliefs have nothing to do with faith or religion. They're what you truly believe about yourself.

What's your story?

Children are born loving and trusting little humans so when an adult tells a child something—it must be true. There is no reason not to believe it. We can't imagine our parents, family members, or any adult for that matter, would lie to us. We believe everything we are told.

Why wouldn't we?

When my two sisters and I were kids, our parents took us on a week's holiday to a seaside caravan park every year. (I use the word 'seaside' very loosely because it wasn't conveniently located next to the beach as you'd imagine. No. It was more like a mile slog to get to the beach. Then another half a mile to reach the water because we always seemed to get to the beach when the tide was out, and I mean way out.)

The park consisted of rows and rows of caravans all neatly lined up like army barracks with a swing set and a sand pit thrown in for good measure. There may have been a law that every British child had their very own sand bucket and spade (but don't take my word for it.)

We never had a say in where we went because our dad was notoriously frugal and quite often traded his mechanic services for all kinds of things—including a week in a caravan for his family. Convenience and location didn't come into the equation at all.

Unfortunately, this arrangement meant that we went on holidays during the offseason, when every other kid in the entire British Isles was in school. I didn't mind being pulled out of school for a week every September. In fact, I quite enjoyed it, but it also meant there were no other kids to hang out with. It was like being on holiday in the *Twilight Zone*. There were no kids—only old people and babies—for miles and miles.

By the time I was thirteen, this caravan park had lost all its lustre (not that it had that much, to begin with.) I was a girl of the world (in my mind at least) and was thoroughly bored with going to the same park every year. Exploring every square inch of it, I had even wandered alone into nearby parks and fields (parent supervision was a bit sketchy in those days.)

With little else to do, I spent most of my free time reading. I read in the caravan. Behind the caravan. Sitting on the swings. Laying in the grass. I even snuck away to read in the back seat of our car. I longed for an exciting life like the girls I read about. I wanted adventure. I even begged my dad to send me to boarding school like the girls in the Enid Blyton books. I wanted to be like my friend Selina, who lived above the bakery before she was sent away to boarding school and I never saw her again (that's a bit suspicious now that I think about it). Anyway, I believed she was living a fabulously exciting life—solving mysteries and hanging out at the stables—while I was stuck at a boring caravan park with two younger sisters and no mysteries to solve.

One morning, as I was lying on the caravan's sofa, deeply engrossed in a book about alien abductions. My dad walked in and said, 'You're so bloody lazy.'

I don't remember if those were his exact words, they may have been part of a bigger conversation. The only thing I know with any certainty is that he called me *lazy*.

Now, I accept that *lazy* isn't a particularly hurtful word (I have been called a hell of a lot worse) but being called *lazy* by my dad felt like a slap in the face.

Perhaps it was because I believed I'd always been there for my dad. When I was eight, I was the one operating the cement mixer when he built a retaining wall between our house and our garage. I was the one who was summoned whenever he needed someone to help him bleed the brakes of the vehicles he was working on. There were times when the coal delivery truck dumped a fresh pile of coal at the bottom of our garden path. (Dad wouldn't pay to get them to physically drop it in our coal shed next to the house because—as I mentioned before—he's frugal and I suspect he traded something for that coal. Custom delivery would surely have been extra.) I hauled the wooden planks to place on the steps for the wheelbarrow. Filled the wheelbarrow with coal. Then pushed the damn thing up the long steep path to the coal shed.

I even carried a brick or two up to my parent's bedroom so that they could raise the bed higher when my mother was giving birth to my sister at home. I was four years old.

Being called *lazy* was something I never expected, and it stung.

Unfortunately, this word uttered by my dad—out of sheer frustration I'm sure—became part of my inner story, and from that day on, I did everything I could to prove that I wasn't lazy. Even though, deep down I believed I was lazy because my dad—a man I loved and trusted more than anyone else in the world—had told me so.

I was an emotionally sensitive child, and the damage was done. Every time I wanted to read, I'd think about everything I should be doing instead. Reading was no longer a healthy activity. It became something I did at night under my blankets with a flashlight. I continued to read in secret and felt guilty about it. It became harder and harder to relax because being lazy was now a part of my inner story.

When you're a child and are told you're not good enough, thin enough, strong enough, pretty enough, smart enough, or you're lazy (thanks for that one, Dad), you may have believed it. I'm not saying this is true for everyone or even that you consciously chose to believe it—but for many of us—these words can become part of our inner story. Sub-consciously, you may think you're not good enough to succeed or be happy. You're not smart enough to get the job promotion so why bother trying. You're not worthy of a better relationship, so you put up with crap or abuse. You're going to fail so what's the point of putting yourself out there.

You may not remember what someone said to you when you were a child, but many people remember those cold, harsh words vividly. They may have been said in jest, in anger or in frustration but either way—when you're a child—they are written in indelible ink on your psyche.

If you were told only positive things as a child, you're one of the lucky ones. Congratulations, your story is probably quite different. Although it's still possible to create a negative story about yourself especially if you felt that you could never measure up to the positive reinforcements you received.

This may sound like I'm blaming parents for screwing up their kids and I suppose I am in a way. As a parent myself, I certainly wasn't perfect. I've said things in moments of frustration that I wish I could take back.

I'm sure my dad didn't realize at the time, that calling me lazy would have such a long-lasting effect. I'm sure he would take it back if he could (at least I bloody well hope that he would.) Unfortunately, you can't take those words back. Like a bullet from a gun, words cut deep. They wound. They can leave a scar that may never completely heal.

What we can do is apologize as soon as we can. Explain why those words were spoken and hope to hell that it's enough to stop the bleeding.

The good news is your story can change over time. Just because you were told something as a child doesn't necessarily mean you still sub-consciously think it's true today.

The bad news is even though you may have had a very positive and loving childhood, it only takes one bad experience with someone to start a negative story.

Examining my personal inner stories was going to be challenging, but I knew it was important because it was these stories that helped create my thinking patterns. Once thinking patterns take root, they can be difficult to tame.

Thoughts create emotions, so I knew I needed to explore my default thinking pattern and find where it came from. How I thought about certain situations was influenced by my thinking patterns. I needed to find out why my default was set a certain way.

If someone tells you to think positively, but your inner story is based on something negative like, 'I'm not good enough' or 'Bad things always happen to me,' trying to think positively about a situation doesn't alleviate what you're subconsciously thinking. Imagine you're a chronic worrier (perhaps you don't have to imagine) and someone tells you 'Don't worry!' Can you turn it off?

Of course, you can't! (If you can, then chronic worry and anxiety is definitely not a problem for you.)

My thinking patterns created constant worry because my inner story was telling me that disaster was waiting around the corner. I couldn't seem to thoroughly enjoy life because something was always lurking in the shadows ready to snatch that joy away. I have no idea where it came from, but it was there all the same. Sub-consciously, I must have believed it. It had become my default thinking because I had trained my mind to go there.

But I should have given my brain more credit.

I never realized it was trying to protect me all along. I was just too blind to see it. Every time I started down the road of negative thinking—my brain sent me a signal. It was frantically waving at me from the sidewalk trying to get my attention, but I just kept my eyes fixed on the road ahead and drove on by.

It often showed up as the annoying, gnawing sensation in the pit of my stomach (worry), and when I ignored it, my brain quickened my heartbeat (doubt) and made my pulse race (fear).

Of course, I kept on driving—ignoring all the signs—blinded by my lack of awareness. It wasn't until I drove smack dab (is that a word?) right into the wall of negativity. Not until it had exploded into full-blown anxiety was I forced to pay attention. By then, the damage was done. The roof had caved in, and I was left wandering around in a daze, trying to pick up the pieces, wondering what the hell happened.

Sometimes our stories are difficult to tell. Sometimes they are buried so deep that you have no idea what they are, let alone how they got there. But ignorance is not always bliss!

My immediate response to the suggestion that I write this book was to laugh and say, "I can't do that!"

This was my default thinking at work, and it was based on an inner story I had about myself. I needed to pause and try to examine why I was thinking that way. It may be because I believed I was a 'nobody.' I didn't have a Ph.D. I wasn't a renowned expert, so how could I expect anyone to listen to me?

What if I can't do it?

What if the book is complete rubbish?

How will I ever recover from that?

The more light I could shine on that inner story, the less I believed it. I soon realized that I could rewrite that story and instead of thinking, *I can't do that*, I started to think *I will write it and at the very least I can say I did my best. That I tried.*

Of course, I still had a fear of failure.

Fear is a normal response when you're stepping out of your comfort zone—and I was taking a giant leap out of mine. Writing a book isn't a life or death decision. I won't shrivel up and die if no one reads it (at least I hope not.)

The more I thought about how it could help other people suffering from anxiety, the easier it became to override the original thoughts of self-doubt.

I may never know the origins of all my inner stories that had ultimately led to my chronic worry, self-doubt, and anxiety. But that's okay because I have no desire to dwell on the past. I don't want to spend my time digging up skeletons for two reasons...

One: I have a very active imagination.

Two: I probably won't like what I find.

It may seem like I'm burying my head in the sand and ignoring my past but I'm a firm believer in leaving the past behind. The past belongs in the past. History has no bearing on what I do from this moment on.

Meditation has taught me that.

My goal over the past few years has been to find a way to rewrite my inner story because the old thoughts were based on my childhood. They were holding me back. They were preventing me from living life to the fullest, and I'm too damn old to be led through life by a child's thinking patterns.

It's too easy to believe the inner story that you're not good enough, or there's no point in trying—so you don't. You may think you are protecting yourself from failure by not trying at all, but that's complete bollocks.

Deep down, we know that don't we?

Taming Crazy

17. Playing the Game

Oh my god, what if this is all on me?

I have never liked games.
Even as a young child, I had no interest in throwing dice and climbing ladders—only to land on a snake and slide all the way back down to square one.

Where's the fun in that? Seriously... where?

There are no solutions to be worked out. No anecdotes to remember or lessons to be learned. It seemed like a total waste of time and *Monopoly* was the worst. I never saw the point of buying all the land you can lay your hands on. Throwing up hotels everywhere and charging everyone exorbitant amounts of money for passing through.

There's no 'Hey, how are you? Let's have a nice cup of tea before you throw that dice again and be on your way.' It's all about who can bankrupt their opponents first and who has the most money in the end. I had no interest in owning hotels, railways or electric companies. I certainly had no interest in going to jail. I just wanted to sit in on the Boardwalk, read a good book and visit with interesting people as they passed on through. I wouldn't even charge them for visiting. (I've been told this kind of attitude will never help me win at Monopoly.)

However, there is one game most of us have played at some point in our lives. There are no rules to follow. No dice to throw. No money to fight over or hotels to buy. Most of the time we're not even aware we're playing it, but we are, and we excel at it. It's called the *Blame Game*, and the rules are really quite simple.

You take no responsibility for anything negative that happens. Blame your parents, your siblings, your loved ones, teachers, politicians, or the world in general for everything that's wrong with your life. The *Blame Game* can be played anytime, anywhere and there's no age limit.

Here's how you play…

Your life would have turned out better and happier if you'd had a better childhood—blame your parents.

You'd be a happier, more trusting person if you hadn't been hurt or let down so many times—past relationships are to blame for that.

You'd be a better parent if you'd had better role models—your parents are definitely to blame for that one.

You'd be a better employee if you had a decent boss or had better equipment or the latest tools and technology—yes, it's your employer's fault.

You'd be happier in your relationship if your partner were more loving, more giving or more supportive—blame your partner, they need to do better.

Isn't this game fun?

When *Dr. Phil* was given his own talk show (after helping Oprah with her nasty bit of business with the cow people), I thought he was brilliant and faithfully watched every show.

I learned how my children's schools could be full of drug dealers, and I needed to watch for signs of drug use. My youngest son says I once checked their arms for needle tracks which I vehemently deny. (Although it does sound like something I may have done once—but I'm still going to deny it.) I learned that pedophiles could be living right around the corner and how easy it was to fall prey to addictions and abuse.

What I didn't realize at the time was that with every episode I absorbed, my worries, fears, anxiety, and obsessive-compulsive issues were escalating.

I watched intently as emotionally drained and mentally exhausted victims described their past. I listened as they blamed their addictions or problems on childhood trauma and abuse. There were times when I would find myself crying along with them as they shared their stories. I told myself that anyone would be damaged by what these victims had lived through.

As human beings, we need to find a logical reason for extreme emotions and behaviours. We need something tangible to blame because it makes it easier for us to understand. But blaming someone or something from our past for our present situation doesn't work. It's merely an attempt to rid ourselves of past pain which is an impossible task.

Playing this blame game—a perfectly understandable and natural response—can keep us trapped in that pain. It becomes almost impossible to find our way out, and we continue to suffer.

I used to be a big believer in the *Blame Game*.

Whenever I read stories of how victims of crimes or the family of someone who had been hurt or killed had forgiven their perpetrators, I never understood it. Even when I learned that you don't forgive for their sake, you forgive for your own peace of mind. I never quite understood why.

In my mind, I would stop at nothing to seek revenge. I would want full justice, and they would pay for what they had done. I would spend the rest of my life in that mindset—grieving for my loss and blaming everyone. Continuing to relive the horror in my mind, whether I wanted to or not.

It has taken me a while to fully grasp what they mean by forgiving others for your own sake. It's the only way out. The only way to end the suffering.

When your inner story has you believing that you are the victim, you become trapped in the victim mentality. It's like the *Blame Game 2.0*.

When you keep identifying yourself as a victim—you keep playing the blame game over and over again because every victim needs a villain!

I didn't realize when I was playing the game. It was never my fault when things went sideways because there was always someone or something I could blame. My early childhood was filled with what I would call *mischievous* behaviour. I could blame it on my parents for not giving me any boundaries, perhaps even being spoilt (although as soon as my sisters came along, that ended abruptly.)

We learn quite early on, how to blame others. We may not say it out loud but sub-consciously, we justify our behaviour by it. Everything we do or say is driven by how we think and feel. If we're feeling frustrated, angry or unhappy, we think it couldn't possibly be our fault—so we find a reason for it. In our minds, the reason is rarely us. It can be difficult to admit you've been playing the blame game your whole life, but it's easy to spot when others are playing.

It may be an occasional 'I didn't do it' or some variation of that. We say, 'I didn't do it' in a multitude of ways.

"What the hell!" I screamed as Ger slammed on the brakes, almost putting us through the windshield and giving us permanent whiplash (this may be a slight exaggeration.)

"Sorry, that idiot almost hit us," he replied. "I guess it would be too much to ask that he signal before cutting us off."

Here's a classic example of how my husband subtly plays the blame game (sorry honey).

I saw *the idiot* signalling to move into our lane. I saw the lane he was in was ending, and he was running out of space to merge—but Ger didn't. If he had seen him, he would have let him in because he's not an asshole. But Ger didn't see him and was now clearly blaming *the idiot* for cutting us off.

On the other hand, *the idiot* was signalling to merge—but when no one let him in—he sped up to pass us and cut us off. He was probably blaming Ger for not letting him into our lane. This is a very basic example, but you can see how easy it is to play this game. You can't lose.

I'm not suggesting that no one is to blame for anything. No, I'm not suggesting that at all because there are lots of people to blame for the crap that goes on in the world. What I am suggesting is that we look at ourselves and see how easy it has become to blame others. It's almost like we do it sub-consciously because we take no responsibility for it when we do.

However, here's a word of warning...

You may not want to point this out to loved ones every time you spot them playing the game. It can go terribly wrong very quickly. Trust me on this.

You may know someone who can't seem to shake off their past and always plays the victim. They probably have no idea they're playing—especially if they've been a victim of something and have played the *Blame Game* for a while. It can become entrenched in their mindset. It becomes their default thinking pattern.

When you stand back and look at all the pieces on the board, it takes no effort to identify the people who are still playing the game. Some players have elevated themselves to victim mentality status, and they're easy to spot if you know what to look for. They have some common traits;

- They constantly complain about other people because it couldn't possibly be their fault.
- They don't take responsibility for anything.
- They are negative about everything.
- They feel sorry for themselves all the time.
- They become defensive quickly, and verbally hit you with force right between the eyes when they feel threatened (metaphorically speaking of course).
- They take pleasure in putting other people down.
- They gossip about everyone and everything.
- They need validation for everything.

"Yes. I'd feel the same way if I were in your shoes."

"Of course, it's normal to think that way."

"Yes, you're right."

We all need validation at times. We all want to know if what we are feeling, thinking or how we're behaving is *normal*. But the people who need validating constantly can wear you down. It's like standing at the edge of a swimming pool watching someone being pulled under. They don't want you to throw them a life preserver or run for help. They want you to jump in the pool with them. They want you to thrash around and experience how they feel. They want you to suffer alongside them because misery really does love company.

We all complain, gossip, be a little negative or needy occasionally (I've done this more than I care to admit.) But when someone is consistently doing these things—when you no longer want to spend time with them or work alongside them—it may be a sign they're trying to mask past pain. They may be stuck in a victim mentality.

At the very least, knowing these signs may give you a better insight into their behaviour. It may help you show more compassion and empathy too (even when they are driving you completely mad, and you just want to poke them in the eye with a stick.)

"I'm devastated," Karen said, as she sat across from me in the crowded coffee shop. Her eyes were red and puffy, and her hands trembled as she reached forward to put her coffee cup down on the table.

"Why? What happened?" I asked.

I first met Karen at our children's elementary school. She was 'Queen of Parent Volunteers' and she wore her crown proudly. She was the mum that other mums wished they could be or the mum you wanted to punch squarely in the face. (I fell into the latter group.)

Perhaps I envied her a little because while she was baking cupcakes for the class and organizing every volunteer event at the school—I was trying to *pull myself together* while juggling my fulltime job, and the boys' hockey practices and games. She always looked immaculate with the latest hair and nails, and her co-ordinating Lululemon yoga outfits, while I often looked like I'd been dragged through a bush backwards.

We were strangers who just happened to have kids in the same class, and that was the extent of our relationship. I hadn't seen Karen in over fifteen years when she bumped into me at a local grocery store—and when I say bumped into me—I mean she literally crashed her cart into mine.

"Al-ee-sha!" she screeched. "It's been so long."

Being called 'Aleesha,' drove me insane but since I didn't expect to see her again—I let it slide.

"Hi, Karen. Yes, it's been a while."

"Do you have time for coffee?" she asked.

Well, this is unexpected.

She had never given me the time of day before. When I took time off work to volunteer in my son's class, she had either ignored me or assigned me to some menial task. I didn't have time for her right now and to be honest, I didn't want to make the time.

"Sorry, I don't right now, I'm in a rush," I said. "What about tomorrow?"

It was just something I said to be nice. I had no idea she would take me up on that offer, but this was the start of our twice-monthly chats over coffee. I wasn't sure I liked Karen all that much. It wasn't as if we had anything in common. We usually spent our time talking about her, but it did feel good to focus on someone else's problems for a change.

It was during our third or fourth meeting that Karen told me her marriage was over. She said she hadn't seen it coming and felt blindsided. But as she talked about their relationship, it was clear that she may have missed the signs. Things like this rarely appear out of the blue, despite what we think.

Their marriage wasn't perfec;t she said, but then no marriage was. They rarely slept in the same bed, and she couldn't remember the last time they'd had sex, but since she didn't feel any sexual desire—and hadn't for a long time—it wasn't a big deal. He had told her that he understood. She didn't worry about it because she knew he wasn't the type of man to have an affair. He had always been a family man and often said that affairs were the ultimate betrayal.

When Karen found out he had been having an affair for the past three years, she didn't believe it at first. She had refused to believe it until he finally told her the truth.

"I can't believe I didn't see it," she said during one of our coffee chats. "How could I have not seen what was happening? How could I be that naïve? That stupid?"

"I don't think you're naïve or stupid," I replied. "I think you may have been in denial, but I also think that's perfectly normal. Nobody wants to believe that someone they've loved, trusted, spent a huge part of their life with, would do this to them. But it happens all the time."

She had tried to make their relationship work, even when her husband had finally come clean with the affair. He told her everything she wanted to know and answered all of her questions. She told him she was willing to try and forgive him. She still loved him. They could move past this—it would take some work to trust him again—but she would try. Perhaps they could go to counselling. But he told her he didn't love her that way anymore. He still cared for her. She was the mother of his children, and he would always be there for her—but not as her husband.

"It won't last," she said, the day he had packed his bags and left the house for good. "He'll be back once he realizes what he's giving up plus she's got two small kids."

I suppose I was her shoulder to cry on. I listened without judgement (well maybe a tiny bit of judgement slid in every once in a while, but I managed to keep it to myself.)

When she found out that they were engaged, her anger turned to sadness. "Where did I go wrong?" she asked.

"When two people get married, they have no idea what will happen. We think love is enough, but sometimes it just isn't," I replied.

"That's the saddest thing I've ever heard. If love isn't enough then every marriage is doomed," she laughed. It was nice to see her laugh again even if it was fleeting.

"I mean it's not enough to just love someone. There's so much more, and both people need to be working at it not just one. We need to meet each other's needs, and even that may not be enough. I guess what I'm saying is that not all long-term marriages are happy and fulfilling. Some people are miserable, but they stay together because they think divorce is this awful thing. Maybe they think it's better to stay together in misery than be looked at as a failure."

"I suppose," she said, staring into her empty coffee cup.

"Times have changed. Divorce happens but instead of looking at it as a failure and blaming each other, look at it as a new beginning. Move on to the next phase of your life—this time on your terms."

I knew it was easy for me to say.

We'd had this conversation so many times before. When she'd found out her kids had known about the affair and hadn't told her.

She talked. I listened.

When she found out they were engaged to be married, and when she was told that they had picked the date—one week after the divorce was final—which also happened to be her birthday.

She cried. I listened.

She had handled it well, or so I'd thought. She had even found a job when she discovered during the divorce that they were not as financially well off as he had led her to believe.

She had moved on.

Now here she was, sitting across from me in a noisy, crowded coffee shop—*devastated*.

"My son doesn't want me at his wedding," she said, breaking the silence.

"He said that?"

"Yes, he did. He said that he didn't want a scene at his wedding. So, I asked him what he meant by that, and he said that he'd talked it over with everyone and they felt it was best that I not go. Apparently, it was obvious to everyone that I didn't approve of 'dad's new wife.' Why the hell do I need to approve of her? She wrecked my marriage and is now having family dinners, holidays, and god knows what else with my kids. She replaced me, and I'm the bad guy." Karen took another sip of her coffee "He said I would make it awkward."

"What did you say?"

"What could I say. I just said, 'Ok fine' and hung up. I've done nothing but cry since then. I can't believe he did this to me. I keep replaying the conversation over and over, and I'm being blamed for everything. That asshole and his wife have turned my kids against me."

I thought about Karen's situation as I drove home. I had always kept a close relationship with my kids and would be heartbroken if anything happened to change that. But was Karen using blame to cloud her judgment?

If every victim needs a villain, it appeared Karen had two—her ex-husband and his wife. She was obviously neck deep in the *Blame Game*.

I had empathy for Karen, but I couldn't help think she had brought some of this situation on herself. She admitted that she didn't hold back the contempt she had for her ex-husband in front of her kids. She had always expressed her hatred for him freely and had blamed him for everything that had happened.

Is it any wonder that her son was concerned about his wedding day? Could he trust that his mum would set aside her feelings for his sake, on one of the most important days of his life?

Karen couldn't continue down this path. She needed to deal with the blame. She needed to accept what had happened and stop playing the victim.

"Can I run something by you?" I asked Ger as I slumped down on the sofa that evening.

"Okay," he said putting down his iPad, a good sign I had his full attention.

"Karen just told me something. She's upset, but I think she's the one to blame for the whole situation. Should I tell her that? In a nice way of course."

"I'm not sure why you're friends with her, all she does is dump her crap on you. Does she even ask you how you're doing?"

"No. You know she doesn't."

I knew this 'friendship' with Karen was one-sided, but I believed it was because she had so many issues and she thought I didn't. I guess she didn't care to ask.

Why was I friends with this woman?

"Okay, so what's the problem this time?" Ger asked.

"Should I tell her that I think she's stuck playing the blame game and that she has the power to change it? She did confide in me, so I think she wants my advice."

"Advice is only welcome if it's asked for, you know that," he said. "She probably needs to hear the truth. If you're willing to risk your friendship, then tell her."

Was I willing to risk our friendship by telling her what I think she needed to hear?

Yes, I was. It wasn't much of a friendship anyway.

But what if I was wrong?
It's not like I was an expert.

I picked up my phone 'Coffee tomorrow?'

18. Sticks and Stones

If you cannot help build them up,
at least don't break them down.

It was a time in our lives when Summer meant dirty faces, skinned knees, and strawberry jam sandwiches.

We spent warm, carefree days building treehouses and exploring new lands. We followed the winding river upstream until we could no longer see our houses in the distance. The river may have only been a meandering stream—but to the two of us—it was the Amazon or the mighty Mississippi.

Philip was a couple of years older than me. Skinny and tall for his age with coal black curly hair that always seemed to fall over one eye. I thought he looked like the boys in the movies.

And I adored him.

We broke chunks of dirt from the riverbank and placed them carefully into the cool, clear water to create a small pool. We worked tirelessly. Until exhaustion wrapped its arms around us, forcing us to collapse into the tall cool grass and stare up at the vast blue sky.

We had planned to build our very own pool that summer. But then Philip mentioned the time we had seen a dead sheep lying in the river upstream on one of our Spring adventures. The sheep had been crawling with hundreds of fat brown wriggling maggots, and I had nightmares for weeks after. We quickly abandoned our swimming pool dream, and although we still washed our dirty hands and feet in the river, we were careful not to splash the maggot water on our faces before running home as soon as the sun went down.

We spent every moment we could playing together.

We were happy and carefree.

Life was good.

At nine years old, I started to sense that something wasn't quite right with Philip, but I didn't know what. There were times when I knocked on his front door, and his mum would say that he didn't feel like playing, or his sister would come to the door and say he was sick.

I wouldn't see him for a few days, and then he would show up at my door as if nothing had happened. He never looked ill, and I never asked. I was just happy to have my friend back.

One morning, after three days of waiting for him to show, I gave up. Grabbing my latest Enid Blyton book, I headed off to our secret treehouse to spend the day alone. Our treehouse was merely a platform made from bits of old wood and corrugated metal sheets that had been left to rot and rust. Hidden amongst the thick brush, it made us feel safe—and best of all—it was our little secret.

No siblings. No friends. No parents. Just us.

I didn't like being there alone, but I pushed my fears aside and sat amongst the dense greenery, trying to ignore the ants, spiders, and the sickly smell of rotting leaves.

"Hi," Philip said, as he suddenly popped his head up through the thick leafy branches.

I sprung up, hitting my head on a low hanging branch.

"Fucking hell," I cried, holding my head with one hand and throwing my book at him with the other.

Fuck was our word.

We knew it was bad. A word only adults and kids much older than us were allowed to say. We knew it was wrong, which was why we only said it when we were alone.

He laughed and climbed in through the narrow opening. Making sure not to dislodge our platform that was wedged in place with nothing but spit, sweat, and blood. I was so happy to see him, that it took all I could do not to hold on to him and never let him go.

Philip picked up my book, and as he reached out to hand it back to me, there was something in his face that wasn't quite right. As he leaned back in his usual place against the tree trunk and closed his eyes, I stared at him. He looked so peaceful. So beautiful laying there that I imagined he would look the same way when he died. The thought brought a telltale twitch under my right eye which always meant a tear was threatening to spill. I quickly looked away.

I quickly glanced back to see if he had noticed me staring, but he was still laying there with his eyes closed and I wondered if he had fallen asleep.

A slight breeze created a small opening in the tree cover letting the sunlight in just enough for me to see his face more clearly. I knew his face well. I studied it when I knew he wasn't looking, but there was something slightly different about it today. A beam of light exposed a yellowish green shadow around his left eye that ran down the side of his nose. It was faded, barely visible, but I knew what it was.

Bruises were our battle scars. You couldn't be a seasoned adventurer like we were without an injury or two along the way. Our knees, shins, and elbows usually had different stages of healing, and we often compared the sizes and colours of them. Blue, black, purple, red, green, yellow—we had seen them all—but the bruise on Philip's face gave me a chill I couldn't shake.

"Where've you been?" I asked. Desperately wanting to know but fearing the answer.

He opened his eyes slowly and climbed back down the tree while I scrambled to catch up with him. We walked along the trail through the woods, threw stones in the stream and soaked our dirty feet in the cold, clear water. Neither of us spoke and as the day wore on—life started to feel normal again. Safe. Comfortable.

"My dad's home," he said, breaking the silence.

I rarely saw his dad. He worked away somewhere, and when he was home, I knew Philip wouldn't be allowed to play. I stayed away and waited.

Philip never talked about him, and I never asked.

"Can you come out tomorrow?" I asked as we reached my front gate.

Please say yes, please say yes.

"Don't know," he said and turned to walk away.

I watched him as he strolled up the street towards his house and disappeared through his garden gate.

The next morning, I rushed to get dressed and ran downstairs for breakfast. Cornflakes with warm milk and a sprinkle of sugar. I quickly rinsed my bowl and spoon, leaving them to dry on the draining-board, and raced out of the house. I knew if I lingered too long, mum would tell me to take my sister along and this would quite literally, ruin my life.

We never told our parents where we were going in those days. As long as we were back before supper 'out to play' was all they needed to know. We never knew where we were going anyway. We let our imaginations guide us. On our rare pre-planned expeditions, we packed jam sandwiches, chocolate biscuits and shared bottles of dandelion and burdock pop, but we hadn't gone on an adventure in a while.

I jumped up on our front garden wall and waited.

We were running out of time. Leaves were starting to change colour—a sure sign that our Summer holidays were coming to an end. Soon we'd be back in school pretending to be strangers again. Philip would ignore me as he passed by with his friends in the school hallway and I would continue to hide my pain. I knew he was embarrassed to be friends with a girl two year his junior. His behaviour hurt, but it was the price I was willing to pay for his friendship away from school.

"Want some Nesquik?" Philip said, startling me.

I hadn't seen him approach and almost fell off the wall, which made him laugh. He turned and started heading back towards his house before I could answer.

This was good. This was very good.

It meant that Philip's dad wasn't home. I also knew it meant Philip's mum, Bev, would offer me a choice of three flavours of *Nesquik*—strawberry, chocolate, and banana—I always picked banana.

Bev smiled as we entered the kitchen. With her coal black hair, short skirts, and bare feet she seemed almost too exotic for our little village. I liked her a lot.

She handed us tall glasses of flavoured milk, and we headed into the living room, settling ourselves on the floor in front of the telly to watch cartoons.

Life was good.

I heard him before I saw him.

A loud deep voice followed by a woman's scream emanated from the kitchen. Suddenly, Philip's dad appeared in the doorway. He loomed over us, holding a handful of Bev's beautiful black hair in his massive fist. She desperately hung on to his belt as he dragged her across the room on her knees.

"Go home," Philip whispered as he pushed me aside and jumped to his feet, spilling his glass of strawberry milk in the process. I stared at the small pink beads of milk as they slowly slid down the side of my bare leg.

Philip lunged at his father allowing Bev a chance to free herself, but his father turned quickly and struck Philip so hard that he fell back against the fireplace hearth. Reaching down, he grabbed a handful of Philip's hair and pulled him to his feet.

Philip's piercing cry filled the room.

Bev hung on to her husband's arm and begged him to let Philip go, but he swung his free arm around and sent her crashing across the room.

Everything was happening so fast, yet time stood still. Nothing seemed real.

I turned to look at Philip. His face white and knotted in pain. When I saw the look in his eyes something in me woke up and I knew I needed to get help. I needed to get out of there immediately. As I ran for the front door, I heard a loud thud and what sounded like a wild animal scream out in pain behind me. I wanted to turn back, but I couldn't. I ran out the door and down the street in bare feet.

I never looked back.

I'll never forget that day because it was the day everything changed. I had witnessed something that Philip had always shielded me from, and it tore us apart.

I suppose it was inevitable and would have happened sooner or later anyway, but I wasn't ready for it. That moment fractured us. Our bond had been broken.

Reality had seeped into our make-believe world, and we couldn't go back—no matter how hard I tried.

I never saw much of Philip after that day. I heard his father had been arrested again, but somehow, he always ended up back on our street. Neighbourhood kids would talk about how they had seen Philip with bruises on his face, but I only saw him from a distance.

We were strangers.

One Sunday evening, as I sat in front of the telly watching *The Wonderful World of Disney,* I heard screaming coming from outside. It sounded like the high-pitched shrieks of a catfight, and I ran to the front window to see what was causing it.

It was already dark outside with winter approaching, but there was enough dusky light from the streetlight for me to see that it wasn't a cat. I could make out the shadowy silhouette of a woman holding on to our front gate, while someone much bigger, was trying to pull her away. I knew without seeing their faces that it was Philip's parents.

The light from out front entranceway suddenly shone a spotlight upon them. I watched my dad run down our front path towards them as Bev desperately hung on to our wrought iron gate as if her life depended on it.

Perhaps it did.

Her bloodcurdling screams trailed off as my dad reached the gate. Her husband released her, turned and ran back towards his house as Bev collapsed on the cold grey sidewalk.

I stared at her as she sank down into our living room chair. She looked like a small frightened rabbit sitting there with streaks of dried dirt on her arms and legs. Bev's beautiful black hair stuck out in all directions as if it was trying to escape, and she had tear stains running through the blood and dirt on her face. She was hurt, but all I could think about was Philip.

I wanted to ask Bev if he was okay, but before I could speak, mum sent me up to bed. I begged and pleaded with her—it was too early, and there was no way I could sleep because I was worried about Philip—but it fell on deaf ears. My mother's friend needed her. Mum had no time for me or my questions right now.

I'm not sure what happened after that night, but I heard rumours that Philip's dad had moved out shortly after. I hoped it was true and that Philip and his family were finally safe.

A year later, I saw Philip while I was on my way to meet some friends at the park. He was leaning against the cement wall of the bus shelter, smoking a cigarette which was pretty much the coolest thing ever to a ten-year-old girl.

He was twelve or thirteen now and was going to junior school, so this chance encounter was the best thing ever. I had so many things to tell him, so many questions to ask but as I got closer, I could see he wasn't alone. Two other boys were lurking in the shadows and suddenly—I didn't feel quite as excited to see him.

"Hi Philip," I said, hoping I sounded more grown up and confident than I felt.

He didn't reply.

One of the boys, who seemed much older than Philip, stepped out in front of me blocking my path. The other one repeated "Hi Philip," in a loud squeaky voice which made them all laugh. I glanced at Philip, but he quickly looked away.

"Is this your girlfriend?" The older boy asked.

"Fuck no. She's just a little bitch that lives by me," Philip said, flicking his cigarette butt into the street.

I fought back the tears.

As I stepped out onto the road to get around the older boy, the other one reached out and grabbed my arm roughly. A sharp pain shot through my shoulder as he shoved me up against the wall with such force that my forehead slammed against the cement.

Holding my arm behind my back with one hand, he plunged his other hand into my trouser pocket and pulled out the few coins he found. From the corner of my eye, I saw his friend approach and soon felt hands all over my body, groping and touching. I felt a rush of cold air as my shirt ripped open. They laughed as I tried to fight back. I kicked and clawed at them, but the more I struggled, the more pain I felt in my shoulder. All I could do was close my eyes and scream.

A rough, callused hand covered my mouth. It tasted like dirt and smelled of nicotine. I pulled my head back just enough and managed to bite down hard and didn't stop until the hand pulled away.

"Bitch."

The grip on my arm loosened and I quickly turned to face them. I tried to push my way through them, but Philip shoved me with such force it knocked me back against the cement wall. I fell to the floor, and they laughed as they turned and walked away.

Clutching the front of my ripped shirt, I sat in the corner of that dark, dirty bus shelter. It stank of stale urine, beer and cigarettes. I felt more alone than ever, and as I sat there listening to the cars pass by, I cried.

I never told anyone about that encounter with Philip and his friends. I was hurt, humiliated, and felt betrayed by someone I thought I knew. From that day on, I did everything I could to avoid him.

Over the next few years, I heard stories about Philip. How he bullied neighbourhood kids. How he took their money and threaten them with violence. In the beginning, I made excuses for him because I suppose I felt sorry for him. But after he broke into our house, I just couldn't defend him any longer.

Years later I heard he was in prison and couldn't help wonder if his dad was in there with him.

I think about Philip every time I hear about bullying.

He was such a beautiful, gentle soul—full of imagination and adventure—yet he lived in a violent world. He was bullied, beaten, abused, and victimized at the hands of his father and it wore him down. It changed who he was and ultimately changed who he became.

They say, hurt people, hurt people.

I think Philip was a classic example of this.

Bullies are not emotionally stronger than their victims, I believe it's quite the opposite. They have a very negative inner story about themselves and have no idea how to process these emotions. They focus that emotional energy into hurting others to try and make themselves feel better. Deep down they're in pain. They're living with a victim mentality and masking their own pain by hurting others.

There is no excuse for bullying, but I do believe there's almost always an explanation.

Bullies are successful when they can tap into someone's negative inner story and exploit it, or they pick on those who can't or won't fight back.

Philip was much smaller and weaker than his father and was much bigger and stronger than me. I guess we were both easy targets.

I can't help but think that if Philip had received proper help—if he'd been shown how to process the abuse he had suffered—then who knows what he could have become.

I had loved Philip.

He was smart and sweet, but I think he felt weak.

I think he had such a negative inner story raging inside him that he punished himself and others for the fact that he couldn't protect his mother—let alone himself.

In those days, there was no such thing as assistance or counselling for victims of domestic abuse. The abuser was removed from the home repeatedly, and that was that.

Every time it happened—Philip and his family were left to pick up the broken pieces by themselves—emotional and otherwise.

Not every victim of abuse will become a bully or an abuser. Some people have a way of processing childhood trauma and creating a better life for themselves. They seem to have the ability to create a better future by choosing the right path and rewriting their inner story. Unfortunately, not everyone is emotionally or mentally equipped to do so.

We need to change that.

19. You're Not Who You Think You Are

Time doesn't change anything,
you have to change it yourself.

Meditation had grounded me in the present—in the only place I could control—and I found it to be a place I was comfortable in.

I no longer felt trapped in fear or anxiety about the future, and there was no blame, guilt, or shame from the past. I also felt more confident in my ability to change the way I thought and felt about all the situations in my life.

Perhaps it was this newly acquired confidence that had me wondering whether I could alter or even erase my existing inner stories and beliefs.

I knew it was my inner stories that had created the most damaging thoughts and I had faith in my ability to manage them. My egotistical thoughts no longer controlled me, but could I prevent my inner stories and beliefs from showing up in the first place?

Or, at the very least, lessen the severity of them?

I wasn't interested in going back and revisiting painful events, and I knew it wasn't going to be as easy as just thinking positively. My inner stories were deeply rooted, and most of them had been residing in my head since I was a child. I had no desire to poke the beehive and risk being stung. *But could I take one of my inner stories and turn it around without jeopardizing all the hard work I'd already done?*

I wasn't sure.

But I'd already come this far and thought I owed it to myself to at least try.

I knew I needed to start with something small, so I started with the inner story I had carried around since I was a young girl— *I was lazy.*

Sub-consciously I must have believed it otherwise I wouldn't still be bothered by it all these years later. I needed to examine this belief and see if I could let it go once and for all. The online dictionary defined the word:

La-zy: adjective
Unwilling to work or use energy.
Characterized by lack of effort or activity.

By that definition, was I lazy?

I loved to lose myself for hours in a good book or lounge on the sofa binge-watching Netflix. But surely that didn't justify the 'lazy 'label.

Looking back, I couldn't pinpoint a time when laziness had been a problem. I'd left home at sixteen and had always worked outside the home even while Ger and I were raising our two young sons. Between working fulltime and having two active boys I was always on the go.

I sure as hell wasn't lazy.

So why was I still carrying it around?

I can only imagine it affected me as it did because it happened when I was thirteen. An impressionable time in any child's life. It also came from my father—a man I had always looked up to. A man who worked six days a week at two jobs. A man who was often exhausted trying to balance work life with being a husband and father to three children. A man who had dealt with life's frustrations and difficulties as best he could I suppose. I didn't know much about my father's childhood, but I knew it wasn't an easy one. So how had he processed his emotional pain?

I had no idea, but it was the probably the same way many of us do. He pushed it aside or buried it. I had never thought that way about him before.

Apparently, my dad was human.

The realization that my father fucked up occasionally just like the rest of us was slightly disappointing yet also quite enlightening.

He had lashed out in frustration and called me 'lazy.' It was time for me to let it go. But how?

How do you let go of a label that had been ingrained in your psyche for all these years?

I couldn't just forget it or pretend it didn't happen because I still remember it vividly. I couldn't remember if I'd eaten lunch most days—but I still remembered that.

I needed to change it.

Dad had been wrong all those years ago. I wasn't lazy. I just knew how to relax—something he had trouble doing himself.

"You were wrong, Dad!" I shouted, startling the dogs but feeling a little better already.

It's funny how we can put our parents on a truth pedestal. We believe they know everything and always have our best interest at heart. Then when we become parents ourselves, we think…

What the fuck?

We have no idea what the hell we're doing. We're winging it—making it up as we go—hoping to hell it all works out in the end. We never stop to think our parents were once in our shoes, or at least I didn't.

I thought about the rocky relationship I'd had with my mother over the years. We'd gone through some rough stretches, and I'd often wondered if we'd survive them.

She was my mother, and I loved her. Yet there were times when I felt she let me down and had not been the mother I thought I needed her to be. I wanted her to be perfect, but I never once thought about her as a real person. I never once thought about how she might be struggling. I never once thought about her.

Could she have been fighting some inner battles too?

Could she have been falling apart right before my eyes?

Was I too wrapped up in my own shit to see it?

Here I was—a grown woman full of all kinds of crazy—and yet I was expecting everyone else not to be.

Damn!

Realizing that we're all a little bit broken (some of us more than others) comforted me for some reason. My family wasn't perfect.

No family is.

At best we're merely pearls—delicate and flawed—strung together with blood and DNA.

Experiences and traumas can break us apart.

Some of us have hairline fractures held together with hope. While others have gaping holes where hope used to live. There are those with emotional wounds buried so far down that they'll never see the light of day.

Shine the light on my pain?

Are you fucking insane?

I knew I had to find the courage to be vulnerable if I was to make any permanent change, but true vulnerability is terrifying. It meant exposing the fragile parts of myself. It meant if I wanted to go all in, I needed to stand naked in the light and trust that I'd survive it. (A bit dramatic I admit, but bloody scary nevertheless.)

I'd always kept my wounds deeply buried, layered with shame and regret. But when I finally found the courage to hold them up to the light, an unexpected thing happened.

They started to heal.

I thought about the hurtful words I had been carrying around all these years. Being called *lazy* was minor compared to everything else I had witnessed, absorbed and buried.

But it was letting go of this one small thing that allowed me to start letting go of everything else.

Being able to look at what had created my inner story with

such clarity and understanding was what I was looking for. It served as validation that I could do this.

I knew I could look at my story, examine it, and not collapse from the weight of it.

20. I Am an Idiot!

Anxiety is never a problem,
until it shows up and becomes a problem.

When I was fifteen, I started to feel like I'd found my place in the world. I felt like I finally fit in with my ragtag bunch of friends who were just as weird as I thought I was. We loved punk music and the fashions that came with it. We pierced each other's ears with darning needles and frozen bags of peas. We snuck out to concerts and danced like we didn't have a care in the world. I loved every minute of it. I felt comfortable. Safe. Loved.

"Your mother and I have something to tell you," Dad said one November evening after supper.

I looked at mum, and she was smiling. I quickly struck death and divorce from the list of possibilities. Staring at dad, I waited for him to tell us we'd won the lottery.

"We're moving to Canada!" He announced, grinning from ear to ear.

Six months later we were on a plane flying across the world. I was devastated.

At the difficult and excruciatingly awkward age of sixteen, I was dragged away from everything I loved. My friends, my boyfriend, family and most of all I was leaving the safety of my familiar, comfortable life. I was heading for the unknown. The uncomfortable, the unfamiliar.

Anxiety soon followed.

Several years ago, my employer asked me to attend an industry-specific university business course. I didn't hesitate. Free education, sign me up. I love learning, and the boss was paying for it—so who was I to quibble? (Isn't quibble an awesome word?)

As I prepared to leave for the first day of the course, the familiar churning started in the pit of the stomach. I tried to ignore it, to push it away, but every time I thought I had knocked it down, it popped back up again. It was like playing *Whack-A-Mole* at the fair.

I checked my email at least eight times (possibly more) in hopes they'd cancelled the course because as we know—cancelled plans are the best plans when you're an introvert with anxiety. No such luck. By the time I was ready to leave the house my mind was racing. I could barely breathe.

For fuck's sake, calm down, stop being an idiot.

As usual, I was overthinking everything but was at a complete loss on what to do about it or how to stop it.

What if everyone there already knows each other?
How will I know where to sit?
What if no one sits with me and I'll look like an idiot?
What if. What if. What if…

Intellectually, I knew worrying about where I was going to sit and who knows who was ridiculous. But intellect had no place here. Little did I know—the worst was yet to come.

First, there was the usual 'Stand up and tell us a little about yourself,' which is enough to make me want to jump out the window or at the very least run to the loo and bunker down there until it felt safe to come out. But even that paled in comparison to what happened next. The instructor walked across the room, dimmed the lights and said, "Okay, if you could bring your attention to the screen we'll begin."

That screen made my blood run cold.

A few days before the course was to start, I had received an email from the instructor stating that all the course participants were required to take an online test. I wasn't familiar with the in-depth *Myers Briggs* test, and although I found a lot of the questions to be total bullshit, I happily answered them and hit the submit button.

Now, projected on the large white screen in the front of the class was a grid with every square representing a Myers Briggs personality. In big, bold letters, the names of all the course participants were arranged in the squares that corresponded to their online test results. Eighty percent of the class were clustered in and around the bottom left corner—representing the extroverted, logical, analytical thinkers—people I didn't understand. The rest were scattered around the middle.

Where the hell am I?

I quickly scanned the overcrowded squares hoping to see my name safely hidden amongst the rest, but I came up empty. It suddenly felt like there wasn't enough oxygen in the room. I looked at the screen again. Out into the wide-open spaces, beyond the populated squares.

And there it was.

My name. Neatly typed. All alone in its own little square far from the crowd. I sat there in horror, wishing the floor would open up and swallow me whole.

Dear god, please take me now!

I had never felt like I belonged. I'd always felt a disconnect from everyone else, but now this feeling had taken a physical form. Projected on the screen like a Hollywood billboard. Here was proof that I didn't fit in.

I couldn't hide it.

I couldn't hide from it.

Sensing my sheer horror, I'm sure, the instructor explained that one of the problems in business is that employers hire people like themselves instead of a variety of personalities to fill different roles. She said something about people like me being the idea people, the creatives, the dreamers, blah, blah, blah… I couldn't hear everything she said because my heartbeat was banging on my eardrums.

It felt like I was under water. Under pressure.

Her words helped to lessen the pain. It softened the blow just a tiny bit, but I still felt incredibly uncomfortable.

And this was only the first morning of class.

How the hell am I going to make it through the rest?

I did make it through and although there were times when I struggled. Times when I felt my heart trying to escape my body. Nothing was worse than how I felt in that first class.

I had always carried around the thought that I didn't fit in and that I was somehow different from everyone else. Not different in a 'you were born to stand out' kind of way, but more of a 'why are you here, you don't belong,' sort of thing.

Could this thought of 'not fitting in' be solely responsible for my social anxiety?

If thoughts create emotions then it was possible—no, it was probable—that my thinking *I didn't fit in* was causing me to feel uncomfortable, or nervous. When I ignored the first sign, my body sent out more—often resulting in full blown anxiety. My social anxiety had become a normal state for me, something that could make me physically sick.

If I changed the thoughts that were driving these emotions, could I ease my social anxiety and even eradicate it?

The thought that I may have the power to do something about it was exhilarating.

I'm an introvert, and perfectly happy with being one.

Give me a choice between staying home or going to a party, and I'd choose a nice cup of tea and a book every time.

But I wanted to have the choice.

I no longer wanted anxiety choosing for me.

If I could change how I thought about social interactions, could I change the way it physically affected me?

The results of the *Myers Briggs* personality test had revealed that I landed squarely into the *INFP* category (I say apparently because I'm always suspect of tests.) Being *INFP* meant I was introverted (obviously), intuitive (nothing too surprising there), feeling (hits the nail on the proverbial head) and perceiving (a big fat yes on that one too.)

INFPs make up only 4% of the population.

Four percent!

No wonder I always felt like I didn't fit in.

Not fitting had always been a substantial part of my inner dialogue but could I be looking at this all wrong?

Did I want to fit in? *Not really.*

Did I want to stand out? *Yes and no.*

I wanted to be unique, but I didn't want to be the principal clown at the circus either. I was different, but I was looking at it as if it was something to be ashamed of instead of embracing it as something good. The more I read about my personality type, the better I started to feel. All these years I had been hiding away the fact that I didn't think like the people around me. I didn't enjoy doing what I believed was *normal.*

But what is normal anyway?

Social anxiety can be debilitating, isolating, and painful. I didn't like interacting with strangers. I looked at certain social situations as something to fear—to avoid if all possible—but what if other people were feeling just like me? If 40 million people were diagnosed with anxiety in the U.S. alone (according to various statistics I'd read on the internet) why did I think I was the only one suffering?

Why did I think everyone else deserved to be there, but I didn't? I was so consumed with my own anxiety; I never once stopped to wonder if I was the only one in the room feeling this way.

That's just what anxiety does.

It makes you feel like you don't measure up. That you're an imposter who always seems to be on the brink of being revealed as a fraud. You're always waiting for that inevitable moment when you're 'found out.'

Perhaps this thought process stems from something in childhood, but it certainly wasn't relevant now. I needed to believe I didn't have to belong, there was no club or group I needed to a part of.

I was unique, just like everyone else.

I needed to stop listening to the voices in my head. Those whispers were responsible for doubting myself. They didn't protect me. They were full of shit, and I needed to tell them to shut the hell up!

With liberation came the desire to prove to myself that I could actually walk the walk, so I signed up to join a local book club.

Normally, I despised my 'let's join something' moments because I almost always regretted signing up for anything—especially when I then had to come up with an excuse not to go. I loathed being the person who never shows up. My desire to go and my aversion to not go was like walking a tightrope between longing and hate.

I had spent my entire life traversing it.

Telling myself that showing up to this book club was only research, made everything seem a whole lot easier (so much so that I might look at my entire life as research from now on.)

As I searched through my closet for something appropriate to wear (which is harder than it seems when you spend your days in yoga pants, not doing yoga), I started to feel the familiar sensation in the pit of my stomach.

I knew this was an opportunity.

It was proof of the process.

Instead of ignoring it, I questioned it because I knew it was my default thinking. My brain was doing precisely what I'd spent a lifetime training it to do.

What are you thinking right now?

I'm scared. I won't know anyone there.

I don't want to go.

Pause. Breathe.

These people are just like me. They love books too.

It's only two hours out of my life.

I've got nothing to lose and everything to prove.

Just breathe.

It's going to be okay.

As I continued to get ready, I kept breathing deeply, letting the air seep into the dark recesses of my gut where anxiety lives. My pep talk seemed to be working, and instead of feeling anxious, I started to feel like I could actually do this.

"What's up with you?" Ger asked as I walked down the stairs, dressed and ready to go.

"What do you mean? I'm going to a book club, I told you this morning."

"Yes, but why are you smiling?"

"I didn't realize I was," I said, grinning as I reached up to kiss him goodbye.

"Have fun."

"You're hilarious," I said, closing the door behind me.

The significance of this conversation wasn't lost on me. Usually, I could come up with at least three different reasons why I shouldn't go. I'd find the best one—the most logical one—and share it with Ger.

"Go or don't go," he'd say, knowing the routine. "No one is forcing you. It's up to you."

I hadn't even attempted to think of an excuse not to go to this book club. The thought of not going did pop up, but it was like a leaf dancing in a breeze and disappeared into the distance. I wasn't feeling nauseous or particularly anxious. Sure, I had some butterflies in my stomach, but instead of labelling it as the start of anxiety—I looked at it as excitement (even though I knew this was a bit of a stretch.)

Perhaps it was nervousness. But considering I didn't feel like throwing up—it was a vast improvement.

My social anxiety had grown over the past few years, and my world had gotten smaller because of it. I told myself I preferred it this way, but the truth was I wanted the choice.

I wanted to decide whether I stayed home or not.

I didn't want anxiety choosing for me any longer.

The book club wasn't great, but I didn't hate it. I didn't keep looking for the exit. I didn't want to hide in the bathroom or feign a migraine so that I could leave without them knowing I was an idiot.

It may have been one small step, yet it was a massive step in the right direction.

Taming Crazy

21. Silencing the Voices

We're human. We fuck up!

'Please call me!!!' Rae's text message didn't give me much to go on, but I knew it must be important if it required an actual phone call and not a text. Rae was an old friend who didn't expect too much from me which is how I liked all my friendships.

The truth is I suck at the kind of friendships that require a lot of energy. I seem incapable of having too many people in my life at the same time. It's not that I didn't care—I definitely cared—but I sometimes had to be reminded that people other than my immediate family needed my attention too.

"Why don't you have friends?" My oldest son asked when he was around eleven years old.

"What do you mean?" I asked.

"All my other friends' mums have parties on weekends."

"Do they?"

"Yes, mum they do."

"I don't like parties."

"Maybe it's because you don't like people."

"Maybe."

This conversation with my son troubled me. It was true I didn't like parties, but I didn't want him thinking I didn't like people. (Even though it was sometimes sort of true.)

He was smart. Intuitive.

Was he picking up on my insecurities and anxieties?

Was I supposed to have friends over all the time?

The thought of throwing a party to prove I had friends did cross my mind, but it evaporated quickly. I was surrounded by people five days a week, seven days a week if you counted the boys' hockey games and practices.

Ger and I liked our family time. It was comfortable. Safe.

Life was perfectly fine just as it was.

We were happy.

Receiving Rae's text message reminded me there were other people in my life—and just like everyone else—she knew I would be there if she needed me. This seemed like that time.

"What's the matter?" I asked when she answered on the first ring.

"I don't know really, I just need to talk. I'm scared."

"Why? Scared of what?"

"I don't know. I just feel like I'm going to ruin things. I don't know how to explain it, I just have this feeling."

Rae had been married to her second husband for less than a year, and she seemed happier than ever. She had divorced her misogynistic, narcissistic, emotionally abusive husband (her words, not mine), after twenty-one years of a miserable marriage and we'd celebrated when she finally left him.

When she met her second husband—who thankfully was the exact opposite of her first—I was so happy for her. She seemed content as they settled in to start a new life together.

Hearing her talk about her fear of ruining her relationship was concerning, but the more she talked, the more it started to make complete sense.

She'd spent over twenty years living with someone who controlled almost every aspect of her life. He had berated her constantly, and that couldn't be magically erased overnight. Her worries, self-doubts, and fears were real and valid, and they had trickled their way back to the surface.

"Can we meet up?" I asked, "I might have something that could help you sort through this."

"I'll come to you," she said.

During her first marriage, Rae had developed some damaging inner stories about herself that she kept hidden. And like many of us, she was still carrying them around. She told herself she should be happy, but perhaps she had the limiting belief that she didn't deserve to be. She was feeling guilty for not being completely happy and afraid of losing what she now had.

It was only a guess, but perhaps her inner stories about not being good enough or smart enough were being echoed by the little voices in her head. They were making her think she didn't deserve to be happy and this marriage would end in failure.

Those thoughts kept percolating. Making her feel like she was undeserving—and because we act on our feelings—it was making her behave differently towards her new husband.

Writing it down, I could see it clearly laid out on the paper in black and white. It made complete sense to me, and I hoped it would make sense to Rae too.

I loved sharing the lessons I learned, but I tend to get too involved and try to 'fix' everything and everyone. Ger reminded me to hold back a little and not jump in with both feet, but I never listened. No, that's not true. I listened. It's just that sometimes his words didn't enter my mind until I had already leaped off the cliff!

This time would be different.

I had no intention of jumping into the pool to save Rae no matter how badly she was drowning. Thrashing around in the water with her would make her feel like she wasn't alone, but it wouldn't help her. I would end up being pulled under with her. No, this time I would be a real friend. Instead of validating her like we all do when we see a friend hurting, I would try and show her a way out. I would stand on the pool's edge and throw her a lifeline and help guide her to safety (at least it would be my intention anyway).

I had read somewhere that empathetic and compassionate people tend to talk about their own experiences when they see other people suffering in a valid attempt to make others feel like they're not alone. Talking about yourself when someone was suffering was called *conversational narcissism*—and although I hated this label—it did sound like something I would do. I needed to control the urge to keep talking and listen.

"He always called me *stupid* especially in front of the kids," Rae said. "Even when we were out with his friends, and I'd say something he'd say, 'It's a good thing she's cute,' and they'd all laugh like it was funny. I'm sure some of the wives noticed what he was doing, but they never said anything."

"Perhaps they were uncomfortable and didn't know you well enough to say something," I said, reaching over to pour her a glass of wine.

"That's true," she said. "He made sure that no one got too close. I could go to work, but he would call several times to make sure I was there. At first, he'd call to say he missed me, but then I realized he was full of shit, he was just keeping tabs on me." She took a sip of wine and settled back into the sofa. "I guess I thought he was the smart one. He took care of the finances, he made all the decisions, and everything we did was because he wanted to do it. I always knew he didn't do anything unless it made him look good. The things he bought were all for show; he probably thought it made him look successful or bigger than he was. We were this perfect little family on the outside, but we were a complete mess. The kids were terrified of him. I told myself that it wasn't that bad because it's not like he was physically abusive, but the emotional abuse was..." she stared off into the distance as if a memory had suddenly reached down and touched her.

Everything Rae said made perfect sense and explained why she felt like she did now. She was upset with herself because instead of being content and happy, she felt unsure and scared.

We talked about how twenty years of an emotionally abusive marriage couldn't be erased overnight. How her self-esteem had taken a severe beating all those years. How she had built default thinking patterns based on all the inner stories she had come to believe about herself. Being called 'useless and stupid' all those years had taken its toll on her.

"Do you think you're stupid?" I asked.

"No, I don't think I am," she said, twisting her empty wine glass in her hands.

"I don't think you are either, but there's a part of you deep down in your subconscious mind that's unsure. You were sort of 'brainwashed' for lack of a better word. You were programmed to believe you were useless and stupid, so even though intellectually you know you're not stupid; I think you still need to deprogram yourself. Re-write your software."

"How the hell do I do that?"

"I'm going to have to get back to you on that," I answered, but I was already formulating a plan in my head.

I thought a lot about Rae's problem over the next few days. I didn't want to rush it because I wanted to make a difference— not only for Rae—but also for myself. I needed to prove that changing our inner story was possible.

Rae's self-esteem had been severely damaged with the inner story that she was 'useless and stupid.' This belief was holding her back and was making her terrified of ruining the relationship she had with her new husband. It wasn't helping her. It was hurting her.

We continued talking over the next few days, and it became clear to the both of us, how she had developed thoughts of inadequacy and self-doubt.

Throughout her childhood, she'd always felt invisible. She

was a middle child who never quite felt like she had a place in her dysfunctional family. She was the quiet one, the one who was never seen or heard. Barely out of high school, she had married someone who told her he loved her for who she was. He promised to take care of her. And even though she didn't really love him, she thought love would come in time. She saw it as an escape from her ordinary, invisible life.

What she didn't see—was that he was damaged too.

It wasn't all bad. In the beginning, he was loving and sweet, especially in public. *Maybe this was what love is,* she thought, although she expected it to feel different. She told herself that this was better than many of the relationships she'd read and heard about.

After their wedding, they moved far away from her family and friends. 'To help build a better life for themselves,' he had said. And she believed him. His co-workers' wives were now her only *friends*, although she never talked to them without him being present.

When she became pregnant, she was thrilled at the thought of having someone to love and share her life with. She poured herself into prenatal books. She made sure she did everything the books told her to do, and she sailed through most of the pregnancy. She was overjoyed at the thought of having a baby, but within days of giving birth to a healthy baby girl, she knew something didn't feel right.

Instead of feeling love, she felt nothing.

She was numb.

Rae didn't know what was happening at the time, but she was suffering from postpartum depression. At first, her husband was supportive but soon, support turned into anger. He told her she didn't deserve to be a mother. She was too stupid to realize that having a baby was the best thing in the world. How could she be miserable when he had worked so hard to give her everything?

She had found her way through by pretending—putting on a brave face—and doing everything she thought a good mother would do. She did what she needed to do so that her husband would leave her alone.

They went on to have two more children, and thankfully she hadn't suffered from postpartum depression as she had with her first child. She settled into building a life for her children while trying to protect them from the angry outbursts her husband often exhibited.

Rae never knew what would set him off. Sometimes it was because she hadn't buttered his toast all the way to the edge, or she'd bought the wrong brand of soup. He lashed out by throwing a glass, a cup, a plate—anything he could lay his hands on. She justified it by saying 'at least he didn't hit her.'

As the years went by and the kids became teenagers, his rage only grew. But she was numb to it. She knew she would leave as soon as the kids were old enough, and that thought was enough to sustain her. She never told a soul about her plan for fear he would find out.

"Remember the day I messaged you and said I'd left him?" Rae said, breaking the silence.

"I do. Ger and I didn't believe it at first. I mean we all knew he was an asshole, but you always looked happy together."

"I know. I guess I was ashamed. I thought it was my fault. I think I'm still dealing with the shame and guilt of allowing my kids to live with that."

"I think we all believe that once we remove ourselves from bad situations, that everything will be great. We don't realize that all those years can do damage and if we don't address it, it just stays there. We can bury it as deeply as we want to, but it's still there. I suppose sooner or later it has to be addressed, or we'd implode."

"And here I am," Rae laughed as she poured herself another glass of wine.

When Rae walked out on her husband for good, she felt free for the first time in her life. But she also felt lost, alone, and frightened. She had found an apartment for herself and the kids. Learned how to balance a bank account and poured herself into her job. She built a brand-new life for herself. When she met her current husband two years later—she was happier than she'd ever been.

Everything was good.

She was good.

Until she wasn't.

Rae's inner story about not being good enough had resurfaced, making her think she was going to sabotage her marriage. She needed to change her default thinking pattern.

But how?

It wasn't as simple as thinking *I am good enough*. If it were that easy, she wouldn't feel like she did now. She needed to believe it.

Over twenty years of hearing the same thing over and over was not going to be erased overnight, but I could try and give her something she could believe.

"I know I'm not stupid," she said when she called the next day "so why do I feel inadequate?"

"I think you know you're not, but there's an inner story there somewhere. A belief you have that you don't measure up. It could have started back when you were a kid and just got reinforced during your marriage."

"That's true. My childhood wasn't exactly a happy one."

"So, let's look at this inner story from where you are right now. You're no longer that timid little kid or that emotionally battered wife. Look at you. You're good at your job, your kids are happy and healthy, and you're married to a great guy. You didn't get to this point because you're stupid or not good enough, right?

"Hell no, I didn't," she said louder than she had intended.

"Exactly. So, let's try and change your inner story to something that's true. Something you believe."

"That makes sense."

"Changing a very negative belief into a very positive one sounds good, but deep down, where it matters, you probably won't believe it. It would be like if someone had always believed they were ugly and then someone came along and said they were gorgeous. They're not going to believe them. But if that person told them something like 'You have beautiful eyes,' they could believe that. I know that's not a great example, but you know what I mean. It's taking a small step in the right direction."

"So, give me an example. What should I believe?"

"What if instead of trying to believe you're 'not stupid' you use something that I use?"

"Should I be afraid? I know what goes on in that head of yours and it's not always pretty."

"Smart ass," I said, happy we could still find a little humour in all this. "This is what I use when I start beating myself up for something, 'I'm human, and I fuck up like everyone else.'"

"I love it. You're letting me have it?"

"We'll share it."

Rae and I talked every few days over the next few weeks. It was good to hear the happiness in her voice. She was feeling better about herself but still had some moments of doubt.

Of course, she did. Change takes time. I kept reminding her that when she was working on changing a belief to try and make sure she stayed present. (This was something I had to remind myself quite often, especially in times of doubt.)

We need to stay in the moment.

We all tend to drift back into the past, but the past no longer serves us. What's done is done, it's out of our control so everything we choose now must be based on the present.

Meditation had taught me that the past only exists in our mind. What we think about our past is the reason we feel pain in the present. Feeling shame, guilt, embarrassment or regret about what we may have done or not done doesn't help.

There are lots of things I wish I could have changed, but it is what it is. Everything I did or didn't do was based on my inner story at the time. We all have the power to wipe the slate clean if and when we choose to.

Every day is a chance at a do-over.

Some people are better equipped to let go of the past. It's something to do with how their brain is wired I suppose. Ger has this ability, and it's something that fascinates me. He doesn't make a conscious decision to let things go, he just does. Self-protection perhaps but I've always envied it.

Changing our inner stories and choosing what we want to believe about ourselves sounds like an impossible feat. But picking the little ones first and getting success with those, makes it all worth it. Tackle the small ones first, and the big ones won't seem quite so big.

Explore your inner stories.

Create new ones.

Make them simple.

Make them believable.

Take the shiny new big ass belief and write it down.

Repeat it to yourself.

Make it your mantra.

Write it on a Post-It note.

Stick it on your mirror.

Stick it on your forehead.

Do whatever works for you, my friend!

22. What's Up, Buttercup?

"The right word may be effective, but no word was ever as effective as a rightly timed pause." ~ Philip Twain

Despite my body's wobbly bits and creaky joints, my inner alarm system was working reasonably well. I no longer ignored the gnawing sensation in the pit of my stomach which had haunted me my entire life.

In fact, I looked at it as something to embrace (okay embrace may not be exactly the right word, but at least I didn't dread it anymore.) I learned to question its existence every time it made an appearance. Changing how I thought about the sensations in my body, even the ones I had despised for so long, meant I was not afraid to feel them anymore. Oh sure, they weren't exactly welcomed with open arms—but when they did show up—I knew it was for a perfectly good reason.

The few times when I did try and ignore it or push it aside, it would throw open the front door and invite all its friends in. Before I knew it, I'd be the uninvited guest trapped in the middle of an anxiety rave.

The *Pause* became everything.

The *Pause* was my weapon of choice, my go-to move, and my saving grace.

That moment between feeling an emotion and reacting to it was the difference between behaving logically (something I'm not entirely familiar with I admit) and acting like a complete loon. The pause stopped me in my tracks and prevented me from making a fool of myself. It gave me a chance to see everything clearly before it created all kinds of havoc. Before it created my own emotional suffering.

Pausing made me look and sound much smarter too. It also meant I needed to apologize for less (trust me on this!)

Here are some of the best times to pause:

One

When someone cuts you off on your way to work. You may feel pissed off because you think *He could have hit me, he knew I was there, what a fucking idiot!* You may have lots of thoughts along those lines.

PAUSE HERE!

You may have already honked the horn, called him/her an asshole and flipped the middle finger because you're human and reactionary, I get it.

PAUSE HERE!

Those thoughts are creating a feeling of anger (if it's rage you feel, you're going to have to work a bit harder on this.) Let those thoughts go and look at the situation again.

Did he cut you off or was he signalling to merge, but you didn't see him? *Possible.*

Did he target you deliberately? *Possible but not probable. (Unless of course, you're an asshole driver yourself and you've pissed him off.)*

Could he have been late for work, or didn't see you, or was frustrated that no one let him in? *Yes, yes, and yes.*

This isn't about you at all, is it? *Nope, it isn't.*

You're allowing a complete stranger's actions to dictate how you feel. You know that, right? *Sigh…*

If your stomach is in knots, you're gripping the steering wheel as if it's a lifeline and your shoulders have quite literally crept up to meet your ears.

PAUSE HERE!

Well, that escalated quickly, didn't it?

Take a breath or two you're going to be okay. But let's not take this emotion along on your journey any further than you need to.

Relax your deathly grip on the steering wheel. Stop trying to strangle it with your bare hands, it's done nothing to deserve that.

Breathe, fill your lungs with air and with every exhale, allow your body to relax.

Breathe, rinse and repeat, until you feel no tension in your face, neck, shoulders or stomach. The only thing you need to focus on is relaxing your body (and the road, of course—let's not forget to focus on the road.)

Arrive at your destination safe and sound—minus your rage and frustration.

Aren't you glad you paused?

Two

When your manager asks you to take on more work, and you want to punch him in the face. Or you want to run and lock yourself in the bathroom and hope he gets tired of waiting and asks someone else.

PAUSE HERE!

You may be thinking that you always do everything. You're the only one that does more than your fair share. Those thoughts are creating your frustration.

PAUSE HERE!

Pause before you complain to co-workers, stop speaking to everyone, or make an ass of yourself.

Pause before you take this feeling home with you and vent to your partner or take it out on our loved ones (not consciously of courses but you know you do.)

PAUSE HERE!

Your manager may have an entirely logical reason to ask you to take on more work. So, pause and look at the situation again.

Do you always have to do everything? *It feels that way.*

Are you assuming no one else was asked? *Probably.*

Have you asked why you're the one they ask? *No.*

Are you assuming instead of asking? *Yes. Yes, I am.*

Are you making this situation all about you? *Sigh...*

This situation needs a great deal of examination because not only do you spend a big part of your day here, but you probably need it to pay your bills. (If you don't, then what the hell are you doing here?)

The places we work can be filled with all sorts of friction. Throwing a bunch of strangers together and expecting them to work all day harmoniously every day is unrealistic and fairly impossible. Sure, most of the time we manage to get through the day without blood loss, but let's face it—a lot of work environments have at least one dick. (Your first task should be to make sure that dick isn't you.)

The point I'm trying to make here is that we create our own drama by what we think about a situation. So, before you make things bigger than they need to be.

PAUSE HERE!

Ask yourself those two little questions before you react.

Is what you are thinking true?

Is your ego playing the starring role?

The answers to these questions can allow you to see the situation a little more clearly and prevent you from making a complete ass of yourself. Try not to take this home with you (or to the mall, or to the bar or anywhere else you may be going after work.)

Breathe and release the tension in your body, unfurl your tightly clenched fists, unfurrow your furrowed brow, and breathe. Deeply.

Of course, if your workplace is a complete nightmare—even without your input—it may be time to part ways. But if you are creating your own drama (we're all responsible for our own thoughts and emotions remember) try and take a different approach.

Try and not take every situation personally, it makes all the difference in the world.

Three

You arrive home from a busy day at work, throw open the door only to be greeted by what looks like the local landfill, and it quite possibly should be condemned?

You feel frustrated, mad, angry, a whole plethora of emotions and not one of them is going to lead to anything good or rational.

PAUSE HERE!

Those emotions you're feeling are created by you—not by the situation—but by all the thoughts that are racing through your head.

Perhaps you think everything is always left for you to do.

No one ever helps you around the house.

Nobody cares about you (come on now Eeyore, you know that's not true.)

PAUSE HERE!

The thing about these kinds of thoughts is that they can be extremely damaging to relationships. They can lead to a feeling of being unloved because we're dealing with family and we have strong emotions when it comes to family.

After all, shouldn't family know how you're thinking and feeling? (No, the answer to that is no.)

Do yourself a massive favour and…

PAUSE HERE!

Make yourself a nice cup of tea before you lose your fucking mind. Go and put the kettle on. Now.

If this situation happens a lot, you may end up screaming

at everyone, saying something you may later regret, slamming doors or crying in your bedroom. Perhaps you're the silent type like me which isn't helpful at all (even though you think you're being all grown up and everything by curbing any physical and verbal outbursts.)

No matter what your reaction, your family will still be surprised by your behaviour. To them, it will look like you've overreacted. Again.

PAUSE HERE!

Before you lose your mind entirely, breathe.

Resist the urge to pack a bag, change your name and run away from it all.

Examine the thoughts that got you here.

Is everything always left for you to clean up? *It looks that way, yes.*

Nobody helps you? *Not unless I scream at them.*

Nobody cares about you? *I might have exaggerated that one slightly.*

There is a lot at play here, but none of it will end positively. The fact you came home to a disaster has nothing to do with you. You don't control how other people behave. Family members can get so caught up in their own thoughts, emotions, and behaviours that cleaning the house is probably not even on their radar—let alone their mind.

It's not a priority for them.

This is not to say they shouldn't clean the house but to only help you understand—this isn't personal.

Make sure you don't assume they know what you need from them. We can all be complete doorknobs when it comes to understanding other people's needs. If you're dealing with teens, you may also be competing with egos and hormones. A deadly combination that usually ends in frustration.

Remember we don't all see things the same way. A complete disaster to you may be perfectly fine to someone else. Especially to many teens who think taking their week-old plates from under their bed is cleaning.

PAUSE HERE!

Communicate what you need from everyone and tell them why you need it. Never forget the why.

The why is everything.

When someone tells you to do something or even asks you to do it—it's much easier to do it when you know exactly why you should do it—and not just because you're told to.

When life throws you a shitty curveball (you know it will) remember to pause, take a breath and look at the situation again.

We're so used to reacting to situations immediately. We rush in head first. Learn to pause—to give yourself a moment to process what has happened—you'll be able to see the situation for what it is, instead of what it appears to be.

That pause can provide you with enough time to look at the situation from the outside looking in, instead of from within your default mindset.

Every situation is different, but the process is basically the same. You can change the result by pausing and examining the thought that's creating the emotion.

There are times when we're not consciously aware we've been thinking about a situation until our body sends us signals to let us know. It rings the doorbell to alert us that we need to pay attention. Maybe it's the gnawing feeling in the pit of our stomach or the increased heartbeat.

These signals mean that we are already feeling an emotion, but we can still pause as soon as we become aware of it. We can pause, breathe and start again.

This makes a huge difference because it means you get to choose whether you stay in that negative emotion or work through it and change it. The reason you feel that emotion is because you weren't conscious of the thought that created it.

Now you are awake.

You're aware of the signal.

You paid attention and get a do-over.

This time you'll be present.

That's the beauty of it.

You are in control.

Just because you weren't aware the first time doesn't mean you can't go back and change it now. Listening to your body is vital because those vibrations are a gift.

Yes, they are. No, really, they are!

They're letting you know you need to wake up from your subconscious and pay attention to them.

Unfortunately, no one teaches us this, so we end up ignoring them, pushing them away, covering them up or fighting them. Our brain sends out more signals, and the more we ignore them, the worse they get. They start piling up, and we suffer the consequences. We end up with anxiety and panic attacks because our body can't process all these emotions or signals that are being sent out at once.

And what do we do?
We suffer.
We self-medicate.
We hide.

As soon as you become aware of an unwanted emotion or behaviour, you need to start over. Go back to the situation and use the T.E.A. process so you can clearly see your thoughts, emotions and actions.

Make sure the situation is a fact and not based on assumption, gossip or your inner story.

Look at the thought.

Is it true or is it based on your ego?

How could you think about the situation now?

The more you practice, the easier it becomes. It will become a habit, and you'll no longer need to examine your thoughts every time because you'll automatically know when you're thinking with your ego, and you'll change how you think about it almost immediately. You'll feel an emotion and instinctively question it.

What the hell was I thinking to create that?

Practice the pause.

It's not the situation that creates your emotions—it's you.

You are your own worse enemy.

But you know that, right?

23. The Good and The Not So Good

It might be a shitty day, but it won't last.
It's already tomorrow in Australia.

You can't talk about worry or anxiety, without mentioning fear. Fear is necessary for our survival.

It's fear that stops us from walking off the edge of a cliff and plummeting to our death. It's fear that prevents us from running up to a big cute grizzly bear or skydiving without a parachute. We call it common sense, but it's origins come from the fear of getting hurt or dying. (Fear of dying tends to be a big motivational factor.)

These days, there are many things to fear, and we allow them into our lives every single day. We are spoon-fed fear through our tellies, tablets, laptops and smartphones.

Fear can be good.

We need a healthy dose of fear to keep us safe. The key words here being *healthy dose*.

Unfortunately, when you spend a hell of a lot of time in the company of worry and anxiety—fear will always show up to the party—whether it received an invitation or not.

The problem starts when we replace our fear with worry. We used to only worry about what happened within the walls of our home, within our community, and what was close by. But now our worry has gone global.

These days we have a plethora of things in the world we worry about. Global warming, gun violence, drugs, gangs, taxes, healthcare, political parties taking away our rights and freedoms, and so much more.

I used to believe that fear and worry were the same thing, but they're not!

Fear is in real time and involves action.

It pops up in dangerous situations and stops you from walking home by yourself late at night when there's a homicidal maniac on the loose. Sometimes we listen to it. Sometimes we don't. But it's a legitimate fear.

Fear is necessary because let's face it—humans can be quite stupid at times. We do stupid things, so to keep us safe we have a fear switch built right in (whether we use it or not is another matter entirely.)

For some of us, the problem starts when we ignore the fear that is necessary, and we replace it with worry and anxiety which is not always necessary.

Not only is worry and anxiety unnecessary in most situations but they also have faulty switches, so we can never turn them off when we need to.

Fear can be over in an instant, but worry—worry includes constant thoughts, sleepless nights, headaches, and stomach issues.

I'd pick fear over worry any day. I just never knew I had a choice. I'm not saying you should never worry (okay I am saying that), but you know what works better than worry?

Concern.

Being concerned about something is like being worried without the side effects. It's like worry's little brother—not as big and likely to hurt you. Concern shows compassion without the needless suffering that follows.

'I'm concerned about this,' is a whole lot better and less stressful than 'I'm worried, and I'm never going to sleep again.' You're not going to stop worrying immediately, but just by changing the word you can help calm your inner chaos.

It's a baby step.

Just take it.

You may have been told that anxiety helps detect and avoid potentially dangerous situations (much like fear), but when you are an anxious person, no amount of anxiety will help.

If you're like me (and I suspect we may have the same propensities since you're reading this), you'll feel much better, lighter, brighter if you ban the word *anxiety* from your lips.

If you've had to battle anxiety for a while, your *fight or flight* gauge may be entirely out of whack. You may have an overactive response to perceived threats. Perceived being the key word there, my friend.

As a child, you may have been told not to be afraid or that you needed to be brave no matter what the situation. You should have been asked what you were thinking and feeling instead.

It would have been helpful to sort out those thoughts that created the worry and anxiety.

It would have been helpful to know being afraid was okay and that it's normal to feel fear.

It would have been helpful to know that fear doesn't hurt us as much as worry does.

Excessive worry can turn into anxiety and cause us a great deal of emotional, mental, and physical pain. Wouldn't it have been great to learn how to process thoughts and feelings as a child and prevent anxiety from becoming a problem in later years? Especially when anxiety is skyrocketing among teenagers, and kids as young as five years old are now being diagnosed with generalized anxiety disorders.

Parents are not totally to blame since they aren't usually equipped with a psychology degree when they decide to populate their little space in the world. (Actually, now that I think about it, its probably in our best interest that they're not.)

So, let's be clear on this one thing.

Fear = Good.

Anxiety = Not so good.

24. What I Know for Sure

Taming: *make less powerful and easier to control.*
Crazy: *full of cracks or flaws: unsound; crooked, askew.*

What I know for sure is that at times when I feel everything is hopeless, when I'm swimming in the depths of despair, and when I feel like time has stopped still—I know that everything will be okay.

The sun will come up in the morning. Spring will eventually come around again (despite what the groundhog says.) Life will continue like it always has and everything will be okay.

What I know for sure is that if I can change the way I think and feel about everything, if I can manage my anxiety effectively that it no longer has a hold over me—then so can you. I'm not saying it's a breeze but my god it's worth it.

What I know for sure is like most things in life, it takes practice to become good at anything—sports, meditation, playing the piano or writing a book (that's a very feeble invitation to cut me some slack here. Is it working?)

Building and strengthening your emotional wellness will have a profound effect on your overall health. You'll navigate life with the clear understanding that you've got this. Of course, you'll experience stormy seas, rugged paths, rabbit holes, and life's inevitable shitty bits. But you will make it through. You'll be okay. At the very least you'll make it through without the prolonged suffering, you're may be used to feeling.

What I know for sure is...
Anxiety is a bitch.
Depression is a bigger bitch.
Anxiety and depression together can be the biggest bitch of them all.

Being in a state of anxiety and depression is not a pleasant place to be, but we can try and help each other climb out of the darkness. We can arm ourselves with the knowledge and skills we need—not only to get ourselves to safety—but to teach the next generation how to prevent falling into that hole in the first place.

It's important to understand that there's nothing fundamentally wrong with feeling negative emotions. Life isn't all about rainbows and sunshine. Shit happens. But some of us can get stuck in a negative loop, and it can become harder and harder to shut it down.

Be aware of that.

Here's a list of twelve things that help get me through life's *WTF* moments:

1. It takes practice to become good at anything, and the changes you've made during this journey are no acceptation. You will falter along the way, but don't give up. Just get up off your ass and keep going.

2. Never underestimate the power of the pause. That pause will give you a chance for redemption. It will stop you from overreacting, making a fool of yourself, and prevent you from falling down that bloody rabbit hole. Make a cup of tea, that's a perfect pause (throw in some chocolate biscuits, and you'll be nailing it.)

3. Raise your standards and cut the toxic loose. Surround yourself with the people you admire, love and respect. Someone once said that 'you become the company you keep,' and although I have no idea who said it initially, or in what context, the message is valid. At the very least, be a better friend to yourself and those around you. Up your game my friend.

4. Labels belong on cans of food, designer clothes, and emotions. Labels don't belong on you. Stop negatively labelling yourself because you will keep living your life depending on the label you give yourself. (I'm still working on the idiot thing.)

5. Use T.E.A. in any situation when you need to understand what it is you're thinking and feeling. Write it down (while you're making tea.) Use T.E.A. to question the thought so you can understand where the

feeling came from. Use it to make better decisions so that you can base a decision on fact instead of ego or emotion. It works, I wouldn't lie to you!

6. Realise that it's not all about you no matter what you believe. Learn to live alongside your ego—not in it. Your ego may always be riding shotgun, but never, ever let it take the wheel. It's a lousy and often dangerous driver!

7. Don't forget to check in with yourself. Life gets so busy, and it's easy to forget to pay attention to yourself. I promise this isn't selfish—it's essential. When your emotional wellness is strong and healthy, you'll be able to help others without draining yourself.

8. Create routines. Every successful person has routines—actions they take every day to keep them on track. It could be something as simple as writing in a journal, a 10-minute meditation, taking a bubble bath at the end of the day, or sitting for half an hour with tea, biscuits and a good book. Healthy routines eventually become healthy habits.

9. You're much more powerful than you think you are. You have a say in how you think, how you feel, and how you act. Choose wisely and stop letting your ego mind control your life.

10. Every day is an opportunity for a new start. If today wasn't such a good day, you get a *do-over* tomorrow. If you fuck up one day, don't drag it into the next. Apologize right now, right this minute and start again.

11. Refuse to be defined by your scars. We're human. We have our own thoughts, emotions, and experiences. Many of us have battle scars to prove it. Your past does not define you, my friend.

12. Forgive. Forgive everyone that may have hurt you—not for their sake—but for yours. Most of all, forgive yourself. Holding on to hate, shame, or guilt is like drinking poison and expecting someone else to die. The only one it hurts is you. Let it go and forgive (it doesn't mean you will forget.) Forgiveness may be difficult, but it's much less painful than hanging on to pain. Trust me on that.

That's a dozen of my main points. Lessons I've learned on my journey from the bottom of the rabbit hole to scrambling back out again. All these things help me navigate my way through life, and I use them every day. They make me a better person, and sometimes I need a reminder to be better. To do better.

We need to experience a wide array of both negative and positive emotions; otherwise we would live in an emotional flatline. It's okay to be pissed off, angry, and frustrated from time to time—but it's not okay to live there.

It's not an emotional state you want to prolong. A negative emotional state may be your default, but you can override it.

Make sure it has a short expiry date and don't get stuck there. Nobody has a say in how we come into the world, but we sure have a say how we live it. No matter what your beliefs are—you are not on this earth to continually suffer—so live your life on your terms.

Happiness is in all of us. Yes, I know it sounds corny and commercial—but no matter how hard I try and refute it—it's still the truth.

It's a waste of your time and energy to keep painful past situations and experiences alive in your mind. Nothing in your past should prevent you from being present now.

Don't give it that power!

Don't spend another moment with constant worry, self-doubt, crippling fear, or anxiety.

You're worth fighting for, so for goodness sake, fight!

25. The Condensed Version

It's hard to appreciate the view when you're
stuck at the bottom of the well.

When you're in the middle of emotional pain or suffering, you may need a quick refresher on what to do right now. Here's a *condensed version* to help get you on the right path.

When you start becoming self-aware, the first thing you may notice is how you are feeling. It may be the knot in the pit of your stomach, your rapid heartbeat or a change in your breathing. Pause and take a deep breath. Let it out slowly.

What exactly are you feeling right now?

Label the emotion. Don't ignore it or push it aside. Face it head-on. Own it. Never be afraid of feeling it. It's only a vibration. It's your body's alarm system. It's there for a reason. Pay attention to it.

When you've slapped a label on it, you're halfway there.
Now pause, take a breath.

What are you thinking?
Get right in your head, wade through the crap and find the thought that's creating that emotion. Ask yourself questions and write down the answers so you can clearly see why your body activated its alarm system.

If you missed all the signs or ignored your body's signals, you may already be at the action stage. Don't worry sweetheart!
It's quite common in the beginning to miss the signs, remember you're new at this. Cut yourself some slack.
You may have always pushed your thoughts and emotions aside. Self-awareness hasn't been your thing, it takes practice. Just remember to pause, take a deep breath, you've got this.

If you find yourself reaching for that second glass of wine, or the bag of snacks, or the bucket of cookies, or you're already facedown in a gallon of ice cream, pause here.
These are all habits that have formed over time. They've helped you cope and have distracted you from not having to deal with your thoughts and emotions.
These actions, habits, behaviours, or whatever you want to call them are a natural response, but they are distractions.
It's like putting a sticker on the dashboard of your car to cover the check engine light so that you don't have to look at that damn light anymore. It might work for a while, but sooner or later you're going to be stranded on the side of the highway wondering why this crap always happens to you.

If you find yourself here, give yourself a break.
   This is a no judgement zone.
   There is no blame or shame allowed here!

We all develop our own ways to cope over the years, a lot of us have had to deal with some pretty heavy shit, so don't start piling on the inner guilt.
   Guilt, blame, and shame is too heavy. You don't need to carry that around anymore, so put it down right now and step away.

Wherever you are in the process, you can stop and pause. Whether you're in the middle of screaming match with a loved one (action), feeling like you're going to throw up on your way to an interview (emotion), or you're thinking about something repeatedly (thought) you can stop. Pause and breathe.

The goal is to identify your TEA right now.
   What are you Thinking? (It's creating your emotion.)
   What is your Emotion? (It's driving your actions.)
   What is your Action? (What are you doing?)

The practice of self-awareness means that you learn to pay attention to where you are in your body right now.

Knowing where you are right now and understanding why you're there, will help you get to where you want to go.
   Sounds a little cliché I know, but it's true—it just takes some of us a bit longer to see it. Even Google maps needs to

know where you are to point you in the direction of where you want to go, and if Google needs to know, you sure as hell do.

When you've paid attention to the signs and signals, hit pause, grab a piece of paper and write it down.

Examine that thought again. Question it.
  Are you making something out of nothing?
  Are you making it all about you?

Keep practicing because I know you can do this.

I'm rooting for you!

Acknowledgements

This book was a lot harder to write than I ever thought it would be. Writing about my personal experiences was not only difficult, but it felt over-indulgent and egotistical. Yet I knew I couldn't write about this topic without sharing a very vulnerable part of myself. I had doubts this book would be of any value, but that's the thing about self-doubt, it's deceptive.

My story will not be your story. Your experience with emotional and mental health will be different from mine. There is no right or wrong, or better or worse when it comes to how much we suffer. It is what it is.

What connects us is the fact we all want to do better, to be better and sharing our stories may help others on their own path. At the end of the day, that's all that matters. When we help others, we help ourselves.

Everything contained in this book is based on my own personal experiences with worry, anxiety, depression, and OCD. Reading other people's stories has always helped me in times of despair, and I hope that sharing my story can help you in some small way.

This book would not have been possible without Ger. The love of my life, the butter on my toast, the gravy on my mashed potatoes. I fucking love you. *Rwy'n dy garu di cariad!*

Throughout this journey, my sister (aka Sista) was by my side. I selfishly dragged her along for the ride (much like the time I dragged her behind the train when we were kids) thankfully, there were no police involved this time. And just like the dragging incident, she swears she wanted to come along, and I love her for that. She was my fiercest cheerleader during the writing of this book and without her, I would never have finished it. Thank you for everything Sista!

To Megan, who happily listened and served as my sounding board of logic. Our in-depth discussions and her daily question, "Did you write today?" motivated me more than she'll ever know. Thank you!

To Carson and Sam, who have enriched my life more than words can say. Thank you for always giving me a reason to laugh. I love you!

To everyone who told me I could do it when I really didn't think I could. To those who listened to my whining and rode the roller coaster of emotions with me. You know who you are. Thank you so very much.

Taming Crazy means a lot to me. I am crazy, it's part of my identity, and I've learned to embrace it. There's a part of my crazy that I love dearly. It's bright and colourful, creative, and full of imagination. But there's also a darker side. It's responsible for most of the emotional pain and suffering in my life, and I have learned to tame it. I'm shining a light into those dark corners.

I'm Taming Crazy.

Resources

Mindfulness in Plain English by Bhante Gunaratana
I can't tell you how many times I have read this book. Whenever I need reminding of what mindfulness means, this is the book I turn to.

The Power of Now and **A New Earth** by Eckhart Tolle
These books can be a bit 'heady,' but no one nails the ego quite like Eckhart Tolle. He is a great reference when you need an in-depth ego check.

Loving What Is by Byron Katie
This book is full of case studies to show you how she uses *The Work* to question your thoughts. Byron Katie is a brilliant resource for helping you understand how to work through any personal issues.

Daring Greatly by Brene Brown
The ultimate voice when it comes to being vulnerable and courageous. Brene Brown propelled me forward when doubt and fear paralyzed me. Vulnerability is hard as hell and Brene walks you through it and makes you believe you really are brave enough. Check out her TED Talk too.

Taming Crazy

Alicya Perreault was born and raised in Wales. She now lives in Calgary, Alberta, Canada with her husband and their two dogs. Previously known as a worry junkie, she blogs about emotional health and wellness on her website.

Taming Crazy – Confessions and Lessons is her first published book.

www.alicyaperreault.com
@alicyaperreault
#tamingcrazy

Notes

Made in the USA
Columbia, SC
05 August 2023

21242462R00148